JOURNEY TO THE CENTRE OF THE EARTH

The *Oxford Progressive English Readers* series provides a wide range of reading for learners of English.

Each book in the series has been written to follow the strict guidelines of a syllabus, wordlist and structure list. The texts are graded according to these guidelines; Grade 1 at a 1,400 word level, Grade 2 at a 2,100 word level, Grade 3 at a 3,100 word level, Grade 4 at a 3,700 word level and Grade 5 at a 5,000 word level.

The latest methods of text analysis, using specially designed software, ensure that readability is carefully controlled at every level. Any new words which are vital to the mood and style of the story are explained within the text, and reoccur throughout for maximum reinforcement. New language items are also clarified by attractive illustrations.

Each book has a short section containing carefully graded exercises and controlled activities, which test both global and specific understanding.

Journey to the Centre of the Earth

Jules Verne

Hong Kong
Oxford University Press
Oxford

Oxford University Press

Oxford　New York
Athens　Auckland　Bangkok　Bombay
Calcutta　Cape Town　Dar es Salaam　Delhi
Florence　Hong Kong　Istanbul　Karachi
Kuala Lumpur　Madras　Madrid　Melbourne
Mexico City　Nairobi　Paris　Singapore
Taipei　Tokyo　Toronto

and associated companies in
Berlin　Ibadan

Oxford is a trade mark of Oxford University Press

First published 1993
This impression (lowest digit)
3　5　7　9　10　8　6　4

© Oxford University Press 1993

All rights reserved. No part of this publication may be reproduced,
stored in a retrieval system, or transmitted, in any form or by any means,
without the prior permission in writing of Oxford University Press
(China) Ltd. Within Hong Kong, exceptions are allowed in respect of any
fair dealing for the purpose of research or private study,
or criticism or review, as permitted under the Copyright Ordinance
currently in force. Enquiries concerning reproduction outside
these terms and in other countries should be sent to
Oxford University Press (China) Ltd at the address below

This book is sold subject to the condition that it shall not, by way of
trade or otherwise, be lent, re-sold, hired out or otherwise circulated
without the publisher's prior consent in any form of binding or cover
other than that in which it is published and without a similar condition
including this condition being imposed on the subsequent purchaser

Illustrated by K.Y. Chan

Syllabus designer: David Foulds

Text processing and analysis by Luxfield Consultants Ltd

ISBN 0 19 585460 8

Printed in Hong Kong
Published by Oxford University Press (China) Ltd
18/F Warwick House East, Taikoo Place, 979 King's Road,
Quarry Bay, Hong Kong

CONTENTS

1	THE MYSTERIOUS PARCHMENT	1
2	ICELAND	11
3	TO THE VOLCANO	19
4	UNDERGROUND	29
5	WATER	38
6	ALONE IN THE DARKNESS	47
7	THE LIDENBROCK SEA	55
8	THE VOYAGE	64
9	ELECTRIC FIRE	73
10	THE TUNNEL	82
11	ERUPTION	90
	QUESTIONS AND ACTIVITIES	101

1

THE MYSTERIOUS PARCHMENT

An exciting discovery

On 24th May 1863, which was a Sunday, my uncle, Professor Lidenbrock, came hurrying back towards his little house at 19 King's Street, one of the oldest streets in the oldest part of Hamburg. The front door was thrown open, footsteps shook the staircase, and the master of the house rushed straight through the dining-room, and into his study.

On his way, he threw his walking-stick into a corner, and his hat on to the table. 'Follow me, Axel!' he shouted as he went past.

Before I had time to move, the Professor called out again, 'Axel! Haven't you got here yet?'

I ran into the study.

Otto Lidenbrock was a professor at the Johannaeum, where he gave lectures on mineralogy. He was a man of learning, and he was both a geologist and a mineralogist. Give him any small piece of rock, and he could instantly say to which of the 600 known types of any mineral it belonged. His name was well known in colleges and scientific organizations all over Europe. Famous scientists like Humboldt and Humphry Davy never failed to visit him when they came through Hamburg. They would discuss their most difficult problems with him.

This, then, was the gentleman who was calling me so impatiently. Imagine a tall, thin man, in excellent health. He was fair-haired, and had a youthful appearance that made him look at least ten years younger than his true age, which was fifty. His big eyes rolled behind his huge glasses, and his long thin nose looked like the blade of a knife. When I add that whenever he walked, he took steps exactly three feet long, and that he kept his fists tightly clenched, as if he was getting ready to hit someone — a sure sign of a man with a temper — you will know enough about him to understand why I always ran when he called me.

My uncle was quite rich, which was unusual, in those days, for a German professor. His house belonged to him, and so did its contents — which included his seventeen-year-old god-daughter, Grauben, who came from the Virlande, old Martha, who was both housekeeper and cook, and myself. Both my parents were dead, and my uncle let me live with him. I was his assistant.

Altogether, life was happy in that little house on King's Street, in spite of the master's impatience — the man could never wait for anything. He was always in a greater hurry than Nature itself. Such a man had to be obeyed. I therefore rushed into his study.

I found my uncle sitting in his big armchair, admiring a large, old book.

'Look at this beautiful book, Axel!' he said. Professor Lidenbrock loved unusual books. 'What a treasure this is. I found it this morning in Hevelius's bookshop!'

The Mysterious Parchment

He said that the book was a valuable manuscript, made in Iceland over 700 years ago. It was not written in the ordinary letters of the alphabet, but in Runic letters, that very few people knew how to read. As he turned over the pages to show me, a small piece of parchment fell out of the book, on to the floor. My uncle seized it.

'What's this?' he cried, carefully unfolding it on his table. The parchment contained about twenty lines of the strange letters.

The Professor looked at the letters for a few moments. Then, lifting his glasses, he said, 'I am sure these are Runic letters. They are exactly the same as those in the book. But I cannot understand what they mean. It must be a very old form of Icelandic.'

Professor Lidenbrock didn't know all the 2,000 languages used in this world but he knew many of them. If he couldn't understand this one, he would certainly lose his temper. I was waiting for it to happen, when the little clock over the fireplace in the study struck two o'clock.

At that moment, Martha opened the door saying, 'Lunch is ready, Professor.'

'Lunch! Don't bother me with lunch!' shouted my uncle.

Martha ran. I ran after her and, without quite knowing how it happened, found myself sitting in my usual place in the dining-room.

I waited for a few minutes. The Professor didn't come. As far as I knew, he had never missed his lunch before. And what a wonderful lunch it was! Soup, eggs, meat and fish, served with an excellent German wine.

My uncle was going to miss all this because of a piece of old parchment! Well, I was his nephew. I thought I ought to eat for him as well as for myself, and so I did.

'Professor Lidenbrock not at the table!' said Martha, shaking her head. 'That means something serious is going to happen.'

I didn't think it meant anything, except perhaps trouble for me, because I had eaten my uncle's lunch.

I had just finished when a voice roared. I leapt from the dining-room and ran to the study.

Saknussemm's puzzle

'It's definitely Runic,' said the Professor, crossly. 'But I cannot understand it. I think it is some kind of secret message, and I intend to find out what it means. Sit down and get ready to write.'

I was ready.

'Now, I am going to call out to you the letters of our alphabet that match these Runic letters. We'll see if that solves it. But be careful not to make any mistakes, I warn you!'

I was as careful as I could be. He called out the letters one after another, and together they formed three lists, each of which had seven words in it. But the words were impossible to understand.

My uncle seized the paper on which I had written, and studied it for a long time.

'What does it mean?' he kept asking himself. 'It's a puzzle, where the letters have been purposely mixed up. Just think! Perhaps in their correct order they will lead us to some great discovery!'

I doubted it but, sensibly, I didn't say so to my uncle. The Professor compared the writing in the book with the writing on the piece of parchment. 'The writing is different,' he said. 'And that double 'm' at the beginning wasn't used in Iceland until the fourteenth century. So the puzzle is at least 200 years later than the book. I think one of the owners of the book must have composed it. But who was he? Now, I wonder if he wrote his name somewhere on the manuscript?'

My uncle lifted his glasses, and examined the opening pages of the book through a magnifying glass. On the back of the second page, he found a few faded letters.

'Arne Saknussemm!' he cried triumphantly. 'That's the name of a famous Icelandic scientist of the sixteenth

The Mysterious Parchment

century. Those old scientists made some amazing discoveries in those days. Why, Saknussemm may have written about one of them in this puzzle!'

The Professor was excited by the idea.

'But why should a scientist want to hide a wonderful discovery in this way?' I asked.

'Why indeed? That's what we're going to find out. I shall neither eat nor sleep until I understand this piece of parchment. And nor shall you, Axel,' he added.

'I'm glad I ate two lunches today,' I thought.

'First,' said my uncle, 'we must try to find the key to the code. That should be easy. The words on the parchment contain so many vowels that they must belong to one of the southern languages of Europe. Saknussemm was an educated man. When he was not writing in his own language, he would have written in Latin. So this is Latin, but Latin in a mixed-up form.'

'Well,' I thought to myself, 'if you can unmix it, my dear uncle, you are a clever man.'

'Let us study it,' he said, picking up the piece of paper on which I had written. 'Here we have 132 letters, Axel.'

But I was looking at a picture on the wall, a picture of Grauben. My uncle's god-daughter was staying with a relative in Altona, and her absence made me sad, for — I now confess — Grauben and I loved each other, and were secretly hoping to marry. Grauben was a pretty girl with blue eyes and fair hair, who was rather serious about everything, but that did not stop her loving me. I worshipped her, and looking at that picture of her carried me into the world of memories and dreams.

I was just thinking about walking hand in hand with Grauben along the banks of the River Elbe, when my uncle banged the table with his fist, and brought me suddenly back to earth.

'Axel!' he said. 'Perhaps all that has happened is that the words have been written down the parchment, from top to bottom, instead of across it.'

He solemnly read out the letters of the words going down the page — first all the first letters, then all the second, and so on — until I had written down many more nonsense words.

I admit that, by now, I was excited myself. I expected the Professor to read out a magnificent Latin sentence.

To my surprise, his hand struck the table. The ink splashed, and the pen flew out of my hand.

'That makes no sense!' shouted my uncle. 'It can't be right!'

He rushed across the study, through the dining room, down the stairs, and out on to King's Street, as fast as his legs would carry him.

The key

Martha ran out of her kitchen as the street door banged. 'Has he gone?' she cried. 'What about his lunch?'

'He won't eat it,' I replied.

'And his supper?'

'He won't eat that either, Martha. Uncle Lidenbrock is not going to eat, and nor is anybody else in this house, until he has worked out the meaning of some old puzzle that is impossible to understand.'

'Oh dear! You mean we will all go hungry, then? The old servant went unhappily back to her kitchen.

I picked up the paper on which I had written the letters.

'What can it mean?' I muttered.

I tried grouping the letters to form words. It was impossible! Although I could find one or two English words, some Latin and French words, together they did not seem to have any meaning.

As I struggled, my brain got heated, and I could not think clearly. I was choking. I needed air. Without thinking, I started fanning myself with the piece of paper.

Imagine my surprise! As the back of the paper was turned towards me each time I waved it in front of my face, I thought I could read more Latin words.

The Mysterious Parchment

Suddenly, I understood. I had found the key! The paper could be read just as it was — but backwards. The Professor had been right — right about the language, right about the arrangement of the letters. Now, chance had shown me how to read them!

I spread the paper out on the table.

'Now let's see what it says,' I said to myself.

Putting my finger on each letter in turn, and going from right to left, I read out the whole message aloud.

What terror it produced! Was what it said really true? Had some man dared to go down into a volcano?

'Oh no!' I cried, jumping up. 'My uncle must never be told about this. If he hears about such a journey, he will want to do it too. Nothing will stop him. He will take me with him, and we shall both die!'

I had never been so worried in my life.

'If my uncle keeps on trying to understand this puzzle,' I thought, 'he too may discover the key. I must destroy it.'

A small fire was still burning in the study. I picked up my notes and Saknussemm's parchment. I was just about to throw them on to the fire, when my uncle opened the door. I quickly put the papers back on the table.

Dying of hunger

Professor Lidenbrock seemed to be able to think of nothing except the puzzle. He sat straight down in his chair, picked up his pen and worked at a mathematical solution for three long hours. He didn't speak, he didn't lift his head. He rubbed out, he crossed out, he started again hundreds of times.

At first, I trembled in case he solved it. But so many different combinations of the letters were possible that there was really no danger.

Night came. The noises in the street stopped. My uncle saw nothing and heard nothing, not even Martha asking, 'Are you going to have any supper tonight, sir?'

The Professor said nothing, so poor Martha went away unanswered. Soon afterwards I fell asleep.

When I woke up the next morning, the Professor was still working. His eyes were red, his cheeks were pale, and his hair was a mess.

I honestly felt sorry for him, but I did not say anything about what I had discovered. I was not a cruel man. Why did I not speak? To protect him.

'I know him,' I said to myself. 'He will want to go. Nothing will stop him. He will risk his life to do something that no other geologist has done. If I show Professor Lidenbrock how to read the parchment, it will be the same as killing him. Let him find out for himself if he can.'

And so I waited. But I had forgotten something.

When Martha wanted to leave the house to go to the market, she could not get out. The street door was locked, and the key had gone. The Professor must have locked the door and put the key in his pocket when he came back from his walk the night before. No one dared to ask him for the key. So there would be no breakfast. I decided to be strong.

At midday, I still stood firm, but by two o'clock I felt really hungry. I started telling myself that the parchment

The Mysterious Parchment

was not so important, that my uncle would not believe anyone had ever gone down into a volcano, that he would treat it as a joke, that we would be able to stop him from going, that it would be better for me to tell him about the secret, than to wait for him to discover it.

At that point in my thoughts, the Professor stood up and put on his hat. What! Would he leave the house, leaving Martha and me locked in, getting hungrier and hungrier?

'Uncle!' I said. 'Uncle Lidenbrock!'

'Eh?' he said, like a man suddenly woken up.

'What about that key?'

'What key? The key to the door?'

'No,' I cried, 'the key to the puzzle!'

The Professor looked at me over the top of his glasses. He could see that I knew something. He seized my arm. His hand became tighter and tighter until I had to speak.

'Read that,' I said, handing him the paper on which I had written, 'read it backwards.'

The Professor cried out. He understood.

Seizing the paper with tears in his eyes, he read out the whole message from the last letter to the first.

It was not very good Latin, but it this is what it said:

> *Go down into the crater of Sneffels Yokul,*
> *Over which the shadow of Scartaris falls,*
> *Before the first of July, brave traveller,*
> *And you will reach the centre of the earth.*
> *I have done this. Arne Saknussemm.*

My uncle jumped as if he had received an electric shock.

'Of course' he shouted, 'of course! Sneffels — that's a volcano on the west coast of Iceland, and Scartaris is the name of its highest point. Sneffels has one large crater, inside which are a number of smaller ones. If we can get there before July, at midday the shadow of Scartaris will be pointing to one of the smaller craters. If we go down that one, we will find the way to the centre of the earth.'

His courage and joy were wonderful to see. He walked up and down, he held his head in his hands, he moved the chairs around, he took some of the rocks from his collection, and threw them in the air playfully. Finally, he calmed down, and fell back, exhausted, into his armchair.

'What time is it?' he asked.

'Three o'clock,' I replied.

'Is it really? I'm dying of hunger. It feels as if I haven't had anything to eat today. Let's have some lunch, and after that ...'

'After that?'

'You can pack my box.'

'What?'

'And your own,' said the Professor, going into the dining-room.

At these words, my whole body shook. To go to the centre of the earth. What a crazy idea! But I decided to say nothing for the moment, and I gave all my attention to the business of eating.

After we had had a good lunch, my uncle spoke to me about his plans.

'Axel,' he said quite gently, 'you are a very clever young man. You shall share the glory we are going to win. But the most important thing is to tell no one about this. I insist on complete secrecy. My rivals in the world of science must not hear about this journey until we return.'

'Do you really think,' I asked, 'that there are any who would risk it?'

'Of course! There are geologists in many countries who, once they knew what Saknussemm had done, would rush to follow his example.'

2

ICELAND

The heart of a woman

When I saw that my uncle had made up his mind to go to the centre of the earth, and that he had also decided to take me with him, I did not know what to think. I decided that some fresh air would do me good, so I left the house, and walked round the town. I reached the Altona road. Perhaps I might see Grauben. Soon, sure enough, she came into sight, walking towards Hamburg.

'Axel!' she said in surprise. 'You have come to meet me.' Then she saw my face.

'What's the matter?' she asked, giving me her hand.

Three sentences later, she knew.

'Axel!' she said. 'It will be a wonderful journey. The right sort of journey for the nephew of a scientist.'

'What Grauben? Aren't you going to say I should not go?'

'Oh no, my dear Axel. And I would gladly come with you if I could.'

How difficult it is to understand the hearts of girls and women! This girl, who loved me, was encouraging me to go on a very dangerous expedition, and she would not have been afraid to come herself. I was amazed and, to tell the truth, ashamed of myself.

'It's still a long time until July,' I thought. 'My uncle may be cured before then of this mad interest in underground exploration.'

It was dark by the time Grauben and I reached the house on King's Street. I expected to find the place quiet, with my uncle in bed as usual. But I had forgotten how impatient he was. We found him outside the house, shouting and waving his arms about among a crowd of men who were unloading goods on to the pavement. Old Martha was running about, this way and that, not knowing what to do.

'Hurry up, Axel!' exclaimed the Professor as soon as he saw me. 'You haven't packed, my papers aren't in order, and I can't find the key to my bag.'

I was horrified. I couldn't speak properly. I could only just whisper, 'Are we going then?'

'Yes, of course. At dawn, the day after tomorrow.'

I ran to my little room.

There was no longer any doubt about it. My uncle had been buying things for the journey. The pavement outside the house was covered with so many rope ladders, electric lamps, axes and other things needed for the expedition, that it would take at least ten men to carry them all.

I couldn't sleep. The next morning, I was called early. I had made up my mind not to open the door, but how could I disobey the sweet voice I heard.

'My dear Axel!'

I came out of my room. I thought that my pale face and red eyes would make Grauben feel sorry for me, and change her ideas.

'Ah, Axel,' she said, 'I see that you have had a good night's rest, and now feel better.'

'Feel better!'

'Axel,' Grauben continued, 'I have had a long talk with the Professor. He is a man of great courage, and you must remember that he is our relative. He has told me about his plans and hopes. He will succeed, I am sure. Oh, Axel! What glory there will be for Professor Lidenbrock — and for his companion! When you return, you will be a man, his equal, free to speak and act as you wish, to ... '

She looked into my eyes and smiled. Her words made me feel much happier.

Still, I refused to believe we were leaving. I took Grauben along to the Professor's study.

'Uncle,' I said, 'Do we really have to go so soon? It's only 26th May and ... '

'Of course we must go now! Do you think it's so easy to get to Iceland from here? There is only one regular boat from Copenhagen to Reykjavik, and it leaves on the 22nd of each month.'

'Well?'

'Well, if we waited until 22nd June, we should arrive too late to see the shadow of Scartaris touch the crater. So we have to get to Copenhagen as fast as we can, to find some other ship. Go and pack!'

Our journey begins

All day, instruments, guns and electrical equipment had been arriving. Poor Martha did not understand what was happening!

'Is the master mad?' she asked me.

'Yes,' I said.

'And he's taking you with him?'

'Yes,' I said.

'Where?' she asked.

I pointed towards the centre of the earth.

'Down into the storeroom?' exclaimed the old servant.

'No,' I said. 'Further down than that.'

Night came. 'I'll see you tomorrow morning,' said my uncle. 'We leave at six o'clock.'

I fell on to my bed. I dreamed wildly about abysses. I felt the Professor's strong hand dragging me into holes so deep that they seemed to have no bottom. I kept falling, going down faster and faster, like a rock dropping through space. My life had become one long fall.

I woke up at five, worn out, and went down to the dining-room. My uncle was at the table, eating a good breakfast. I looked at him angrily but, as Grauben was there, I said nothing. I ate nothing, either.

At half past five, a carriage arrived to take us to the station in Altona. Soon it was filled with our luggage.

My uncle solemnly handed the keys of the house to Grauben. She kissed her godfather calmly, but she could not stop a tear or two as her sweet lips touched my cheek.

'Grauben!' I whispered.

'Go, Axel dear, go,' she said. 'When you come back, I shall be your wife.'

I held her in my arms, and then got into the carriage. From the door, Martha and Grauben waved goodbye. The driver whistled, and the two horses began to pull the carriage along the road to Altona.

At half past six, the carriage arrived at the station, and at seven o'clock we were sitting opposite each other on the train, with all our luggage. The whistle blew, and we were on our way.

I watched the changing scenery. My uncle checked his pockets and bag, to make sure he had brought all the right papers. I noticed the piece of parchment among them, and cursed it from the bottom of my heart.

Three hours later, the train arrived at Kiel. From there, we went by ship to Copenhagen, where we arrived at ten in the morning, on 28th May, and went straight to a hotel.

After a quick wash, the Professor was off again, taking me with him. Up and down the harbour we went, in search of a ship to Iceland.

I hoped we would not find one, but I was disappointed. A little Danish ship, the *Valkyrie*, was sailing to Reykjavik on 2nd June. The Professor was so pleased that the Captain was able to ask double the usual fare. 'Come on board on Tuesday, at seven in the morning,' he said, putting the money in his pocket.

'What luck!' my uncle said to me. 'Now, let's have some breakfast, and see the sights of Copenhagen.'

I explored the city like a child. What delightful walks we could have had there, my pretty Grauben and I, beside the harbour and along the green banks. But Grauben was far away, and I would never see her again.

Mr Fridriksson helps

The morning of 2nd June arrived. We had letters, written by famous scientists, to give to several important people in Reykjavik, including the Governor of Iceland, telling them who we were.

Our precious luggage was taken on board the *Valkyrie*. A few minutes after we got on board, the ship sailed out. In an hour, she was through the straits between Denmark and Sweden, and moving into the Kattegat. Towards evening, the ship went round the northern point of Denmark, and during the night, sailed along the southern coast of Norway and entered the North Sea. Two days later, we saw Scotland. Soon after that we reached the Atlantic, and it was hard sailing.

I was quite well on this voyage, but my uncle was sick from beginning to end. This annoyed him, because instead of being able to question the Captain about Iceland, he had to stay in his cabin.

On 11th June, we passed Cape Portland, the most southern point of Iceland. And on 13th June, we arrived in Faxa Bay, off Reykjavik.

The Professor came out from his cabin at last, pale, but as eager as ever. He dragged me forward, and pointed at a high mountain with a double peak to the north of the bay.

'Sneffels!' he cried. 'Sneffels!'

We climbed down into a waiting boat, and were soon on Icelandic soil.

The first man we saw was the Governor. The Professor handed him his letters from Copenhagen, and the Governor offered his ready help. My uncle was also kindly received by the Mayor of Reykjavik and Mr Fridriksson, a science master at the Reykjavik school. This delightful man took us to stay at his house.

'Well, Axel,' my uncle said to me. 'The worst is over.'

'Over?' I exclaimed.

'Why, yes. Now we have only to go down.'

'But when we have gone down, we still have to come up again.'

'Oh, I am not worrying about that — it's getting down to the centre that is the important thing.'

We had lunch at the house of the friendly schoolmaster, Mr Fridriksson. Professor Lidenbrock ate well after his unhappy days on board ship.

Conversation was in Icelandic, but my uncle included some German, and Mr Fridriksson some Latin, so that I should understand. They talked about the library in Reykjavik, which my uncle had visited that morning.

'What books,' Mr Fridriksson asked my uncle, 'did you hope to find in our library? I may be able to help you.'

I looked at the Professor. He hesitated about replying, but decided to speak.

'Mr Fridriksson,' he said, 'I want to find the works of Arne Saknussemm.'

'Arne Saknussemm!' replied the Reykjavik teacher. 'You mean the sixteenth century scientist who was also a great traveller?'

'Exactly.'

'His works are one of the glories of Icelandic literature and science.'

'I see that you know him well.' My uncle was delighted. 'But what about his books?'

'Oh, his books. There aren't any.'

'What — not in Iceland?'

'Not in Iceland, or anywhere else.'

'Why is that?'

'The government did not like the things he wrote, and in 1573 all his books were burnt.'

'Excellent! Splendid!' cried my uncle, to the horror of the Icelandic school master. 'That explains everything. Now I see why Saknussemm had to hide his secret.'

'What secret?' asked Mr Fridriksson.

'A secret which ... whose ... '

'Have you some secret Saknussemm paper?'

'No ... er ... no, I was just guessing.'

'I see,' said Mr Fridriksson, and kindly changed the subject. 'I hope you won't leave our island without seeing some of its mineral wealth.'

'No, indeed,' replied my uncle, 'but I imagine other scientists have been here before me.'

'They have, Professor Lidenbrock. But there is still plenty to see.'

'Do you think so?' asked my uncle, with an innocent air.

'Oh, yes. There are so many mountains and glaciers and volcanoes still to be studied. Look at that mountain over there, for instance. That is Sneffels.'

'Ah!' said my uncle. 'Sneffels.'

'Yes. One of the most interesting volcanoes, with a crater which is seldom visited.'

'Is it dead?'

'Yes, it has been inactive for over 500 years.'

'Well,' said my uncle, crossing his legs to stop himself from jumping into the air. 'I think I should like to start my studies with that Seffel ... Fessel ... What do you call it?'

'Sneffels,' replied the good Mr Fridriksson.

This part of the conversation had been in Latin, so I had understood it all. I could hardly stop myself from laughing aloud at my uncle's efforts to hide his plans from Mr Fridriksson.

'You have given me an idea,' my uncle now told the schoolmaster. 'We shall try to climb that mountain, and perhaps even study the crater.'

'I am very sorry indeed that I can't come with you,' said Mr Fridriksson.

'Oh no! Oh, no!' my uncle replied quickly. 'Thank you very much, but we wouldn't wish to disturb you.'

'How do you expect to get to Sneffels, though?' asked our host.

'By boat, I suppose, across the bay. That's the shortest route.'

'That's not possible. There are no rowing-boats in Reykjavik. You will have to go by land, following the coast.'

'Good. I'll get a guide.'

'I can suggest one. He is a steady man. A hunter who lives near Sneffels — and who speaks perfect Danish, too.'

'When can I see him?'

'Tomorrow, if you wish.'

'Why not today?'

'Because he won't arrive until tomorrow.'

'I'll see him tomorrow then,' sighed my uncle.

3
TO THE VOLCANO

'A splendid man'

When I woke up, my uncle was talking loudly in the next room. I got up and joined him.

He was speaking in Danish to a big, strong man with blue, intelligent eyes, and long, red hair. You could see immediately that nothing could disturb such a man. He stood there with his arms folded, listening to all my uncle's excited talk, but showing no signs of excitement himself. When he wanted to say 'No', his head turned from left to right. When he wanted to say 'Yes', it bent forward, so slightly that his long hair hardly moved.

I would never have guessed that such a large man could be a hunter, but Mr Fridriksson explained that he hunted only one type of bird, for her fine, soft feathers, and that the bird really did the work for him, since she pulled out the feathers herself.

This hunter, called Hans, was to guide us to the village of Stapi, at the bottom of Sneffels. We would start on 16th June. The journey would take seven or eight days. My uncle, myself and our luggage would go by horse. Hans would walk.

On arrival at Stapi, Hans would continue to work for my uncle as long as he was needed, on condition that he was paid three silver dollars every Saturday evening.

Never was an agreement reached so easily.

'A splendid man,' said my uncle as soon as Hans had gone.

'So he's coming with us to ... '
'Yes, Axel, to the centre of the earth.'

It was already 14th June, and we spent all day packing our things.

Instruments were put in one pack: thermometer, manometer, chronometer, compasses, telescope, lights. Guns were in another: two rifles, two handguns. Tools were in a third: axes, hammers, iron bars, ropes ...

Food was in a fourth pack, enough food to last us for six months. The only liquid, however, was gin. There was no water at all. My uncle expected to find underground springs, and we would fill our water-bottles at those.

In addition to all this, we had medicines, tobacco, money and six pairs of tough, waterproof boots.

'We should be able to go a very long way,' said my uncle.

The next day, 15th June, we finished our packing. Our host, Mr Fridriksson, gave my uncle a fine map of Iceland, and we passed the evening in pleasant conversation with him.

I slept badly that night, and at five in the morning I was woken by the sound of horses. I dressed quickly and went down into the street. There, Hans was loading the last of our luggage. My uncle was giving more advice than help, but Hans took little notice of him.

At six, everything was ready. Mr Fridriksson shook hands with us. My uncle thanked him gratefully in Icelandic. I thanked him in my best Latin. Then we got onto our horses.

From Reykjavik to Stapi

Hans, quick and untiring, walked ahead. The two pack-horses followed him, and my uncle and I rode behind them.

Outside Reykjavik, Hans took a path along the coast. We rode between poor fields that were more yellow than green, and saw nothing except a few cows and sheep. The hills to the east were hidden in mist. Now and then, patches of snow glittered on the slopes of distant mountains.

To the Volcano

I smiled at the sight of my uncle, such a tall man, on his little horse.

'Good horse! Good horse!' he kept saying. 'You will see, Axel, that there is no animal more intelligent than the Icelandic horse. Snow, storms, rocks, glaciers — nothing can stop him. As long as we don't force him, we shall do thirty miles a day.'

'We may, but what about the guide?'

'Oh, people like that can walk for miles, without even noticing it.'

Two hours after leaving Reykjavik, we reached the little town of Gufunes. Here, Hans stopped and shared our simple breakfast, answering my uncle's questions about the road with only 'Yes' or 'No'.

We continued on our journey, and did not stop again until four in the afternoon, when, having travelled twenty miles, we reached Hvalfjord. The fjord, a long, narrow strip of sea running inland, between steep cliffs, was over two miles wide at this point, and its waves crashed against the sharp rocks.

'If these horses are really intelligent,' I said, 'they won't try to cross this fjord.'

But my uncle, impatient as ever, tried to force his animal into the water with shouts and blows until, finally, it threw him off.

'There's a ferry,' said Hans.

'Why didn't you say so before? Let's go,' said my uncle.

'We must wait for the tide to turn,' said the guide.

My uncle stamped his foot. It was six o'clock in the evening before the tide was right, and it took two men over an hour to row us across.

At half past seven, we reached Gardar, where we were to sleep for the night.

It was still light because, in Iceland during June and July, the sun never goes down below the horizon. Nevertheless, the temperature had fallen. I was cold and very hungry by the time we stopped at the house of a poor farmer.

The master of the house shook our hands, and led us straight along a passage to the visitors' bedroom, which had a floor of beaten earth and two wooden beds covered with dry hay.

He asked us to join him in the kitchen, the only one of the four rooms with a fire. When we walked in, the host, his wife and their children all said, 'Be happy', kissed us on the cheek, and bowed low. Then we sat down to supper. It was strange food — dried fish and sour milk — but I was hungry, and I ate and drank it all.

At last, I was able to get into my bed of hay.

At five o'clock the next morning, we said goodbye to our host, and gave him some money that he didn't want to take.

Now the way became wetter and more lonely, with few animals and even fewer people. We crossed several little fjords, and spent the next night in an empty hut.

During the third day of our journey, the scenery was the same, but by night-time we were half of the way to Stapi.

On 19th June, we walked on a floor of lava for three or four miles, and here and there we could see steam rising from hot springs. Soon the ground was wet beneath the horses' feet. We were travelling west now along the top of Faxa Bay, and the two white peaks of Sneffels appeared in the clouds less than five miles away.

I was beginning to feel tired, but my uncle stayed as fresh as the day we left Reykjavik. To our guide, of course, the journey was nothing.

On the evening of Saturday 20th June, we reached Budir village on the sea-shore, where my uncle paid Hans as they had agreed. We stayed with Hans's family that night, but next morning we rode on. We were very near Sneffels now, and the Professor never took his eyes from it.

'So that,' he seemed to be thinking, 'is the giant I am going to defeat.'

We travelled on all the next day, getting closer and closer to the volcano all the time. We stopped for the night in the village of Stapi. The following day we did not travel, but got everything ready for our long journey into the earth.

Now my uncle had to explain to the guide that he intended to explore the inside of the volcano. Hans didn't mind. It made no difference to him whether he went across his island, or down into the heart of it. That evening he arranged for three Icelanders (instead of the horses) to carry our things as far as the bottom of the crater.

I had forgotten my fear during the excitement of the journey, but now it seized me again. Above all, I worried that Sneffels might not really be extinct, and that a new eruption might happen at any moment. I told my uncle what I feared, but he would not listen. Sneffels, he said, had not been active for over 500 years, and there was nothing to be frightened of.

I felt beaten. I had only one hope left — that when we reached the bottom of the crater, we would find no passage. But I had a terrible dream that night, in which I was shot into space from the depths of an erupting volcano.

Climbing Sneffels

The next day, 23rd June, Hans was waiting for us with three companions. He had added one leather bottle full of water to our luggage. That, plus our own bottles, would give us enough water for a week.

It was nine o'clock in the morning. My uncle paid our host all the money he demanded, and we left Stapi.

Sneffels is 5,000 feet high. From our starting-point I could not see its two peaks against the grey sky. All I could see at the top was snow.

Led by Hans, we walked behind one another along paths too narrow to walk side by side. Conversation was impossible.

I had plenty of time to observe the country through which we were passing. The more I saw, the more confident I became. The rocks were so clearly volcanic, so clearly caused by great fires coming up from inside the earth, that no one would be foolish enough to try to go below the surface.

The way became more and more difficult. The ground was rising. Pieces of rock kept breaking off, dangerously.

Hans walked over the rising ground as calmly as if it were level. Sometimes he disappeared behind great rocks, and then a high whistle from him told us which way to go.

After three tiring hours, we had reached only the base of the mountain. Here, Hans ordered a stop, and a little food was shared out for breakfast. My impatient uncle ate his quickly, but the stop was meant for rest, too. He had to wait another hour before the guide gave the signal to continue. The three Icelanders were just like Hans — they said nothing, and ate very little.

Now we began to climb the slopes of Sneffels itself. The top seemed to be close, but it took us many hours to reach it! Loose stones kept rolling down at high speed. Sometimes, the cliffs were so steep that we couldn't climb them at all and had to go around. We helped each other and used our iron sticks at these difficult places.

Fortunately, after the first hour of climbing, we came to a sort of volcanic staircase. It served us well. By seven in the evening, we had climbed the 2,000 stone steps to the point where the main Sneffels crater began.

The sea stretched away 3,200 feet below us. We were above the snow-line, which is not very high in Iceland. It was cold and windy, and I was very tired. My uncle, in spite of his impatience, decided to stop and called the guide. But Hans shook his head. He thought it unwise to spend the night there. So we continued our climb. Round and round, backwards and forwards. It took us nearly five hours to climb the remaining 1,800 feet. I was weak from cold and hunger, and I could not breathe properly at such a height.

At last, at eleven o'clock that night, in complete darkness, we reached the top of Sneffels. Before going down into the crater to shelter from the cold wind, I saw the midnight sun shining on the island below.

The shadow of Scartaris

The next day, we awoke half frozen by the sharp air, but in bright sunshine. I got up from my stone bed to enjoy the magnificent scene.

I was standing on top of the southern peak of Sneffels. From that point, the view extended over most of Iceland. Below me were deep valleys, lakes looking no bigger than ponds, rivers no bigger than streams. To my right, in the east, there were glaciers — huge areas of ice, slowly moving down the mountains sides — and also snow-covered peaks, which looked like waves on a stormy sea. To my left, towards the west, stretched the ocean itself.

It was hard to see where the land ended and the water began. I lost myself in wonder, delighted at the great height, forgetting the dark abyss that we would soon be going down.

Hans and the Professor joined me.

'Here we are at the top of Sneffels,' said my uncle, 'and here are the two peaks. Hans will tell us what Icelanders call the one on which we are standing.'

'Scartaris,' said Hans.

My uncle looked at me triumphantly.

'Now for the crater!' he cried.

The crater of Sneffels was about one mile across at the mouth. I estimated its depth at 2,000 feet, but the bottom measured not more than 500 feet all round, so the way down was quite gentle.

I thought of the thunder and flames the crater had contained, and might contain again. But I could not go back now. Hans set off in front again, and I followed him without a word.

We walked slowly down around the inside of the cone, among the loose rocks. In some places, there were glaciers, and here Hans advanced with great care, using his iron stick to test the ground. At certain points, we had to fasten ourselves together with a long rope so that, if one person slipped, the others would save him.

By noon we had arrived. I looked up and saw the mouth of the cone circling a patch of sky, with the peak of Scartaris rising into space.

At the bottom of the crater we could see three smaller craters. These were chimneys through which, during its eruptions, Sneffels had sent out its lava and steam from the furnace below it. Each was about 100 feet across. I did not dare to look into them, but Professor Lidenbrock ran rapidly from one chimney to the other, waving his arms about, and muttering to himself. The Icelanders and I sat on blocks of lava, watching. They clearly thought he was mad.

Suddenly my uncle shouted. I thought he had fallen in. Then I saw him with his arms stretched out in front of a granite rock in the centre of the crater. He looked amazed, then wild with joy.

'Axel! Axel!' he cried. 'Come here! Come here!'

I ran over to him. The Icelanders didn't move.

'Look,' said the Professor.

Sharing his amazement, if not his joy, I read on the rock the cursed name.

'Arne Saknussemm!' cried my uncle. 'Have you any doubts now?'

I didn't reply. Overcome by this piece of evidence, I returned sadly to my lava seat. I knew then that nothing would stop my uncle from going ahead with his plan.

When I lifted my head again, only my uncle and Hans remained at the bottom of the crater. The three other Icelanders had been dismissed, and were on their way back to Stapi.

Hans was sleeping peacefully at the foot of a large rock while my uncle circled the bottom of the crater like a trapped animal. I had neither the desire nor the strength to get up so, like the guide, I went to sleep. But I did not sleep well. I imagined that I could feel the floor of the crater trembling.

That was our first night inside the crater.

Next day, the sky over the cone was grey and cloudy. I noticed this not so much because of the darkness inside the crater, but because of my uncle's anger.

I understood the reason for it, and hope grew again in my heart. Let me explain.

Of the three ways down into the earth, Saknussemm had taken only one — the one on which, according to the parchment, the shadow of Scartaris fell during the last days of June. Now, if the sun failed to shine, there would be no shadow. It was 25th June. If the sky remained cloudy for another six days, the expedition would have to wait until next year.

The day went by, and no shadow appeared on the bottom of the crater. Hans did not move from his place, although he must have wondered what we were waiting for — if he ever wondered about anything. My uncle did not speak to me once. He only looked at the sky, in helpless anger.

On 26th June, there was still no sun. It rained all day. Hans built a hut with blocks of lava, and I quite enjoyed studying the noisy little waterfalls running down the inside of the cone. My uncle was desperate.

On 27th June, the sky was still grey. But heaven always mixes joy and sorrow, and Sunday 28th June brought a change in the weather. The sun shone into the crater. Every rock and every stone had a shadow. The shadow of Scartaris stood out sharp as a blade and moved slowly with the sun.

My uncle moved with it.

At midday, it gently touched the edge of the middle chimney.

'It's there!' cried the Professor. 'It's there! Now for the centre of the earth!'

I looked at Hans.

'Forward!' said the guide calmly.

'Forward!' replied my uncle.

It was thirteen minutes past one.

4
UNDERGROUND

Down the chimney

The real journey was beginning. So far, it had just been hard work. From now on, there would be difficulties at every step.

I had not yet looked down into the pit, but now the time had come. Hans was so calm that I was ashamed of my fear. I thought of my pretty Grauben, and walked across to the middle chimney.

I leaned over a rock and looked down. My hair stood on end. I felt faint. If Hans had not pulled me back, I should have fallen.

All the same, I had seen the inside of the chimney for a moment. Its walls were almost vertical. Plenty of lava lumps stuck out for our feet to step onto, but how should we balance? The staircase was there, but the rails were missing! A rope fastened to the top of the chimney might help us on our way down, but what would happen when we came to the end of the rope?

My uncle solved the problem. He took a rope which was 400 feet long and as thick as a thumb, passed it around a block of lava, and threw both ends down the chimney. We could each descend holding both halves of the rope. When all three of us were 200 feet down, we could pull on one end of the rope, and repeat the performance as often as necessary.

'Now,' said my uncle when he had finished, 'each of us will carry one pack on his back. Hans will take the tools and one third of the food. You, Axel, will take another third of the food, and the firearms, and I will take the instruments and the rest of the food.'

'But who,' I asked, 'is going to carry the clothes and this pile of ropes?'

'They will go down by themselves.'

'What do you mean?'

'You'll see.'

My uncle liked action. On his instructions, Hans tied the clothes and ropes in a single bundle, and threw them down the chimney. I heard a loud rush of air. The Professor leaned over the edge, watching the bundle disappear from sight.

'Good,' he said. 'Our turn now.'

Was it possible to hear these words without terror?

We each put on our packs, and the descent began. Hans went first, then my uncle, then me. The silence was disturbed only by loose stones crashing into the abyss.

I let myself down, seizing the double rope with one hand, and steadying myself with my iron stick, which I held in my other hand. The rope seemed too thin to bear the weight of three people. I used it as little as possible, and my feet gripped the lava bumps as if they were hands.

'Be careful!' said Hans quietly, every time one of these slippery steps shook under his feet.

'Be careful!' repeated my uncle.

After half an hour, we reached a large rock that was firmly fixed to the wall of the chimney. Hans pulled one end of the rope, and the other end came down from the top, in a rain of stones and pieces of lava.

I still couldn't see the bottom of the chimney.

Half an hour later, we had descended another 200 feet by the same method.

No geologist, surely, would have tried to study the surrounding rocks at such a time. I certainly didn't. But the Professor seemed to be observing things because, at one stop, he said to me, 'The further I go, the more confident I feel. These volcanic rocks show that the famous English scientist Humphry Davy is right. He refuses to accept the idea that heat rises from the centre of the earth to the surface. He says it works the opposite way round, and that the heat in volcanoes is caused by certain minerals, like potassium and sodium, mixing with air and water. He proved it to me once when he visited me, you know. I am sure, now, that we will find that the central parts of the earth are quite cool.'

I felt no desire to argue. Everything he saw made him more determined than ever to go on. He mistook my silence for agreement, and the descent began again.

After three hours, I still couldn't see the bottom of the chimney, although the opening at the top was growing smaller all the time. It was gradually getting darker.

We had now thrown the rope fourteen times. Each separate descent took half an hour, and each time we took a quarter of an hour's rest. Altogether, we had been climbing down the chimney for ten and a half hours. With fourteen descents using a rope 200 feet long — that meant we must be 2,800 feet down.

At that moment, Hans called out, 'Stop!'

I stopped just before my feet hit my uncle's head.

'We have arrived,' said the Professor.

'Where?' I asked, slipping down beside him.

'At the bottom of the chimney.'

'Is there no other way out, then?'

'Yes, I can just see a sort of tunnel sloping away to the right. We'll look at it tomorrow. Let's have our supper now, and then sleep.'

It was not yet completely dark. We ate, and then lay down on a bed of stones and lava. At the top of the chimney, as if at the end of a giant telescope, I could see a bright star. Then I fell into a deep sleep.

10,000 feet down

At eight o'clock the following morning, a ray of daylight woke us up. It was reflected and multiplied by the lava walls, and was bright enough for us to see surrounding objects.

'Well, Axel, have you ever spent a more peaceful night in our little house on King's Street? No city noises here, eh?'

'Oh, it's certainly quiet enough down this chimney but it's also rather frightening.'

'If you're frightened already,' cried my uncle, 'what will you be like later? The pressure here is only twenty-nine inches. This chimney only goes down to about sea-level. So far we haven't gone even a single inch into the earth itself ... Now, where is that bundle you threw down ahead of us, Hans?'

'Up there,' said the guide, pointing to a lump about a hundred feet above us. As easily as a cat, he climbed up to fetch it.

'Good,' said my uncle. 'Now let us have breakfast. Remember, we may be going on a long journey.'

We swallowed our biscuits and meat with a few mouthfuls of water mixed with gin.

Then my uncle took a little notebook out of his pocket. He studied his instruments one after another, and recorded the following information:

> *Monday 29th June*
> *Time: 8.17 a.m.*
> *Pressure: 29 inches*
> *Temperature: 6° C*
> *Direction: east-south-east*

The compass direction referred to the dark tunnel my uncle had pointed out last night.

'Now, Axel,' exclaimed the Professor with pleasure, 'we are really going to descend. This is the exact moment at which our journey begins.'

With these words, he lit our two electric lamps and gave one of them to Hans to carry. Now we could see properly, and would be able to for a long time.

'Forward!' cried my uncle.

Each of us picked up his own pack. My uncle entered the tunnel, which went down into the earth at a steep angle. He was followed by Hans, pushing the bundles of clothes and ropes in front of him. I looked up and saw for the last time, at the top of the chimney, that Icelandic sky. I would never see it again.

The tunnel sloped down at about forty-five degrees. Fortunately, lava had forced its way along during the last eruption in 1229, and now this made useful steps under our feet. The lava shone too, reflecting our electric light. On the walls, it formed coloured stalactites, and quartz crystals hung from the ceiling like lamps that seemed to light up in welcome as we passed.

'It's magnificent!' I cried. 'What a sight, Uncle! Don't you admire the colours of that lava? And those crystals?'

'Ah, you're beginning to like all this, are you, Axel? Well, you'll see even finer sights, I hope. Quick march!'

It would have been more accurate to say quick slide, because we were simply slipping down steep slopes.

The compass, which I kept looking at, pointed steadily south-east. The lava steps went straight down for as far as we could see, turning neither to left nor right.

The temperature did not seem to be rising much. I kept looking at the thermometer, and two hours after we entered the tunnel, it only showed 10°C. This made me think our descent was more horizontal than vertical — but the Professor would know, because he kept measuring our depth.

At about eight in the evening, he ordered us to stop. The word stop was music to my ears, as we hadn't stopped for seven hours. Hans spread out some food on a block of lava, and we all ate hungrily.

We were in a sort of cave, where there seemed to be plenty of air, even a gentle wind. I was too tired to think about it, but one thing did worry me — our supply of water. My uncle was expecting to find underground springs but, so far, we had seen none.

'We have only enough water for five more days,' I told him.

'Don't worry, Axel. We shall find more water than we need, as soon as we get beyond this lava.'

'But the lava may extend a long way. I don't think we have gone down very far yet.'

'Why do you say that?'

'Because if we had, it would be much hotter.'

'That's your idea,' replied my uncle, 'but what does the thermometer say?'

'15°C, which means a rise of only 9°C since we entered the tunnel.'

'So?'

'Well,' I said, 'the temperature underground is thought to rise one degree every 125 feet, at least. Let us calculate from that.'

'Calculate it then my boy.'

'Easy,' I said, writing some figures in my notebook. 'Nine times 125 feet is 1,125 feet. So we have gone down 1,125 feet.'

'According to my observations,' said the Professor, 'we are 10,000 feet below sea-level.'

'Impossible!'

'Perfectly possible, or figures aren't figures any more!'

The Professor's calculations were correct — we had already gone 6,000 feet deeper than the deepest mine in the world. Yet, instead of being over 80°C, the temperature was only 15°C. Very strange. It began to look as if Humphry Davy's theories were correct.

Returning to the surface

The next day, 30th June, at six in the morning, we went on down the lava tunnel. It now sloped quite gently.

At 12.17 p.m., Hans stopped.

'Ah!' said my uncle. 'We have to make a choice.'

I looked around. The tunnel had divided into two passages, both equally dark and narrow. Which should we take? It was difficult to decide.

My uncle did not want us to think that he was hesitating. He pointed to the eastern passage, and soon all three of us were in it.

The slope was now very slight. Sometimes, the passage opened up into a wide hall with a high ceiling, like the inside of a large church. Sometimes, it was so low that we had to bend our heads, or even crawl.

The temperature was still perfectly comfortable. How hot it must have been, though, when the lava rushed along this route!

'I hope,' I thought, 'that the old volcano doesn't decide to start again while we're here.'

I didn't say anything to Uncle Lidenbrock. He wouldn't have understood my fears. His one idea was to go on, and he walked, slid and even fell, but I had to admire the way he allowed nothing to stop him.

At six in the evening, after a fairly easy day, we had travelled five miles south, but hardly a quarter of a mile down. My uncle told us to stop. We ate without much conversation, and went to sleep without much thought.

Our arrangements for the night were very simple: a blanket each, in which we rolled ourselves. After all, we had neither cold nor visitors to fear.

We awoke next day feeling fresh and cheerful, and continued our journey along the lava. The passage, however, was becoming horizontal. I thought perhaps it was even rising slightly. At about ten o'clock in the morning, we were definitely going up, and I had to walk more slowly.

'What's the matter, Axel?' the Professor asked impatiently.

'I'm tired.'

'What? When we've nothing to do except go down?'

'I'm sorry, Uncle, but you mean go up. The slope changed half an hour ago. If we go on like this, we shall return to the surface.'

The Professor shook his head, not wanting to hear. I tried to say more, but he gave the signal to go on. I hurried after Hans, who was following my uncle. It would be terrible to lose them.

Still, if we were going up, we were getting nearer the surface. I might see my little Grauben again, soon!

At noon, the walls of the passage changed. The rocks that we were passing through were arranged in sloping layers. They belonged to the Silurian period in the earth's history. We were leaving the lava and the very old granite for newer rocks! We were going the wrong way!

'Look!' I said to my uncle, pointing at the different kinds of rock.

'Well?'

'We have come to rocks from the period when the first animals and plants appeared.'

I made the Professor shine his lamp on the walls, expecting him to show surprise. He did not say a word. He simply walked on.

Had he understood me? Did he refuse to admit that he had chosen the wrong passage? It was clear that we had left the lava route, and that this way could not lead to the furnace of Sneffels. Perhaps I was placing too much importance on the change in the rock. Perhaps I was making a mistake myself.

'If I am right,' I thought, 'I shall soon find some evidence of primitive plants. I must keep my eyes open.'

Within a hundred yards, I found the proof I was looking for. We were no longer walking on lava, but on a dust composed of plants and shells. Professor Lidenbrock must have noticed, but he still walked on.

I could not bear it any longer. I picked up the complete shell of a small animal, and ran forward to my uncle.

'Look at this!' I said.

'Yes, it's a shell, Axel. We have left the granite and the lava route. I may have made a mistake, but I cannot be sure until we reach the end of this passage.'

'I understand that, Uncle, and I would agree to going on — if we weren't in increasing danger.'

'What danger?'

'We have very little water left.'

'In that case, Axel, we must drink less.'

5
WATER

'Our only problem'

It was indeed necessary for us to drink less. Our supply of water could not last for more than three days, as I realized that evening at supper.

All the next day, we walked almost without a word.

The rock glittered in the electric light, and there were magnificent examples of coloured marble. I noticed the fossils of more advanced creatures than I had seen yesterday. We were climbing the ladder of animal life.

Professor Lidenbrock seemed not to notice. He was waiting for one of two things to happen: for a gap to appear at his feet, which we might continue our descent down, or for something to block our way. Evening came and neither hope had been satisfied. That night, I began to feel thirsty.

On the Friday, we set off again, along the winding passage. After walking for ten hours, I noticed that the walls of the passage were no longer made of marble. They were made of coal instead.

'We are in a coal mine!' I exclaimed.

'A mine without any workers,' replied my uncle.

'Oh! Who knows?'

'I know,' replied the Professor. 'I am certain that this passage was not made by human beings. It's time to eat. Let's have supper.'

Hans prepared some food. I ate hardly anything, but drank the few drops of water I was allowed. Half of the guide's bottle was all the water that remained for three men.

My two companions stretched out on their blankets and slept. I could not sleep, and counted the hours until morning.

At six o'clock on the Saturday morning, we started again. Twenty minutes later we reached a cave so huge that I realized my uncle was right. This mine could never have been dug by human beings. We were, in fact, the first people ever to enter it.

What a story those dark walls told! I thought about the period, all those millions of years ago, when coal beds were formed. I thought about all the mineral wealth we were passing through. I forgot to be tired.

This journey through the coal mine lasted until evening. My uncle became more impatient. We could never see more than twenty yards ahead, so we could never estimate the length of the passage.

Suddenly, at six o'clock, a wall appeared before us. To the right, to the left, above or below, there was no way through. We had come to the end.

'Good!' cried my uncle. 'Now at least we know. We are not on Saknussemm's road, and there's nothing we can do except turn back. Let us have a night's rest. In less than three days we shall be back at the place where the tunnel divided.'

'Yes,' I said, 'if we have the strength.'

'And why shouldn't we have the strength?'

'Because by tomorrow we shall have no water.'

'And does that mean we shall have no courage either?' asked the Professor, sternly.

I did not dare to reply.

We started early on the Sunday morning. By the end of the day, we had drunk all the water. After that, we had nothing to drink except gin, which burnt my throat so that I hated the sight of it. I was very tired. More than once I nearly fainted. Then the others would stop and try to help me. But I could see that my uncle was suffering, too, from tiredness and thirst.

At last, at 10.00 a.m. on Tuesday 7th July, crawling on our hands and knees, we arrived back at the point where the tunnel divided. I dropped onto the lava floor.

Hans and my uncle, sitting against the wall, tried to eat a few pieces of biscuit. I fell asleep.

After a while, my uncle came across and held me in his arms.

'My poor nephew!' he said kindly.

I was not used to tenderness from the stern Professor. I seized his trembling hands in mine. He looked at me with tears in his eyes, then he put his water-bottle to my lips.

'Drink,' he said.

Had I heard properly? Was my uncle crazy?

'Drink,' he said again, and I drank.

What sweetness I knew at that moment! Just one mouthful of water, but it was enough to save my life.

'Dear Uncle!' I whispered, with my eyes full of tears now.

'That's all there is, you understand. I kept it carefully at the bottom of my bottle, Axel, I kept the water for you.'

'Thank you! Thank you!' I repeated, as some of my strength came back. 'But now, Uncle, as we have no water, we must return to Sneffels. May God give us the strength to climb to the top of the crater again!'

'Go back?' said my uncle, almost to himself.

'Yes, go back. Immediately.'

There was rather a long silence.

'So, Axel,' said the Professor in a strange voice, 'that water I gave you didn't bring back your courage and energy?'

What sort of man was this?

'What, you don't want to return?'

'And give up this expedition, just when it may succeed? Never!'

'Then we must be prepared to die?'

'No, Axel, no. You must go back. I don't want you to die. Hans will go with you. Leave me here alone.'

'Leave you here!'

'Leave me, I tell you. I have started this journey and I shall either finish it or never return. Go, Axel, go!'

I went across to Hans and put my hand on his. He did not move. He knew how much I had suffered, but the Icelander gently shook his head, and calmly pointing to my uncle, he said, 'Master.'

'Master?' I cried. 'You're mad. He isn't the master of your life! We must go back! We must take him with us! Do you hear me? Do you understand?'

I had seized Hans by the arm and was trying to make him get up, when my uncle interrupted.

'Calm yourself, Axel,' he said. 'Hans is too faithful a servant to do what you ask. So listen to what I suggest.'

I folded my arms, and looked straight at my uncle.

'The lack of water,' he said, 'is our only problem. In the eastern passage of lava and coal, we found none at all. If we follow the western passage, we may be more fortunate.'

I shook my head, as if I couldn't believe what I heard.

'Let me finish,' the Professor went on. 'While you were lying here asleep, I looked at that western passage. It goes straight down. In a few hours, it will bring us to granite, and there we are sure to find plenty of springs. I know it, and I am asking you for only one more day. If, after one day, I have not found the water we need, I promise you that we shall all return to the surface.'

What an effort it must have cost my uncle to make such a decision! I could not say no to him.

'All right,' I said, 'we will do as you wish. But we have only a few hours left. Let's go!'

An underground river

The descent began again, this time following the western passage. Hans went first as usual. We had not walked a hundred yards before the Professor, shining his lamp along the walls, cried, 'These are very old rocks! Now we are on the right path! Forward!'

The twisting passage we had entered was formed in the early days when the earth was becoming cooler, and gaps and hollows had been made in the rock.

Here and there, lying between the layers of rock, parts of which were a splendid shade of green, we could see threads of copper and gold. Riches hidden for ever from the greedy eyes of men!

Next we came upon glittering white mica. So bright was the light reflected from our lamps, that I felt as if I were walking inside a huge, hollow diamond.

At about six o'clock in the evening, this festival of light came to an end. The walls grew darker. The mica joined with other minerals to form the hardest rock of all, the rock that carries the weight of the whole earth. It felt as if we were in a huge prison of granite.

It was now eight o'clock, and there was still no sign of water. I was wild with thirst. My uncle marched on, always listening for the sound of a spring. My legs began to fail. I tried to keep walking so that he should not have to stop. That would drive him to despair, for the day was nearly over — the last day that he had.

But finally I cried out and fell.

'Help! I'm dying!'

My uncle turned back. He looked down at me with his arms folded.

'It's all over,' he muttered.

His expression of rage was the last thing I saw before I closed my eyes.

When I opened them again, I saw my two companions lying rolled up in their blankets. Were they asleep? I could not sleep, I was suffering too much. My uncle's words — 'It's all over!' — echoed in my ears. It was hopeless. I was so weak there was no way of returning to the surface.

We had four miles of the earth's crust above us, and all its weight seemed to be on my shoulders. I felt crushed, as I tried to turn on my granite bed.

A few hours passed. The silence was like the silence of death. No sound could reach us through walls so thick.

Yet I thought I heard a noise. It was growing darker in the passage, and then I saw the Icelander going into a nearby tunnel, taking his lamp with him.

Why was he leaving us? Was he abandoning us? My uncle was asleep. I tried to shout, but no sound came through my dry lips. It was now completely dark, and silent again.

'Hans has abandoned us!' I cried to myself. 'Hans! Hans!'

After my first fright, I felt ashamed at being suspicious of such a man. And in fact, Hans was not going back up the passage, he was going further down it. Had he discovered something? In the silence of the night, had he heard something that I had not?

For a whole hour I tried to decide why our quiet hunter had left us. The strangest ideas entered my mind. I thought I was going mad.

At last I heard footsteps deep down. Hans was returning. A light began to shine on the walls, and then it came round the nearest corner. Hans appeared.

He went over to my uncle, put his hand on his shoulder and gently woke him up.

'What is it?' asked my uncle.

'Water,' said Hans.

'Water! Water!' I cried, clapping my hands and waving my arms, as if I really were mad.

'Water!' repeated my uncle. 'Where?'

'Down below,' replied Hans.

Down below! I squeezed the guide's hands in thanks, while he looked calmly at me.

We got ready quickly, and were soon going down a steep hill. Half an hour later, we had travelled a mile and a quarter, and were 2,000 feet deeper into the earth. We had found no spring, and I was frightened again.

At that moment, I heard a sound like distant thunder through the granite walls.

'Hans was not mistaken,' said my uncle. 'That noise is the roar of a river.'

'A river?' I asked.

'No doubt about it. An underground river is flowing around us.'

We hurried on, full of hope. I no longer felt tired. The sound of running water had already refreshed me. The river, which had been over our heads, was now leaping along inside the wall on our left. I kept touching the rock to see if it was wet, but I could feel no water.

Another half an hour passed. We had walked another mile and a quarter.

We realized that the guide had gone no further than this during his absence. He had heard the water in the rock, but he had not seen it or drunk it.

Hans stopped at the point where the river seemed closest. I sat near the wall. I could hear water rushing violently past about two feet away, but a granite wall still separated us from it.

The Hansbach

I sighed heavily, without trying to think of any solution. Hans looked at me, and I thought I saw him smile. He stood and picked up his lamp. He went up to the wall. He pressed an ear against the dry stone and moved slowly backwards and forwards, listening hard. I realized that he was trying to find the exact spot where the noise was loudest. He found that spot three feet above the ground. Excited, I hardly dared to guess what he intended to do.

He seized his axe, and I knew.

'We are saved!' I cried.

'Yes,' said my uncle, equally excited. 'Hans is right! What a splendid guide he is!'

Nothing, of course, could be more dangerous than to use an axe. This rock supported the world. What if the wall fell and crushed us? What if the water, bursting through the rock, carried us away? These were real dangers but, at that moment, we were so thirsty we didn't care.

My uncle and I would have been in too much of a hurry to strike the rock properly. Hans was calm and controlled. He struck it lightly until there was an opening six inches wide. I imagined the water on my lips.

After an hour, the axe had gone two feet into the granite. I was twisting with impatience, and my uncle was just picking up his axe to join in, when water suddenly shot out of the hole.

Hans, almost thrown over by the shock, could not stop a cry of pain. When I put my hands in the water, I shouted out, too. The spring was boiling hot!

'This water is boiling!' I complained.

'It will soon cool down,' said my uncle.

The passage was filling with steam, and a stream was forming.

Soon we were able to drink. What pleasure! What joy! What was this water, and where did it come from?

We didn't care. It was water and, although it was still warm, it brought us back to life. I drank, without stopping, for a whole minute.

'There's iron in it,' I then said.

'Fine!' answered my uncle. 'Then this expedition will be good for our health. I suggest we give Hans's name to this life-giving stream.'

'Agreed!' I cried, and the stream was immediately named Hansbach.

Hans didn't take any notice. After a short drink, he sat down in a corner in his usual quiet way.

'Now,' I said, 'we mustn't let this water run away.'

'Why not?' asked my uncle. 'I expect the supply goes on for ever.'

'Nevertheless,' I said, 'let's fill the bottles, and try to stop up the opening.'

Hans, however, couldn't close the hole he had made in the wall. The pressure of the water was too great.

'I've got an idea,' said my uncle.

'What?'

'Why are we so anxious to close the hole?'

'Because ... ' I could not actually think of a reason.

'Then let's allow the water to run on! It has to run downwards, and it will guide us, as well as refresh us, as we go.'

'What a splendid idea!' I exclaimed. 'With the stream to help us, there's no reason why our expedition shouldn't succeed.'

'So you're beginning to think like I do, my boy!' laughed the Professor.

'Not just beginning — I already do!'

'Wait a while, though. We need a few hours' rest before continuing.'

I had completely forgotten that it was night, although the chronometer now reminded me. Soon all three of us fell pleasantly asleep.

6

ALONE IN THE DARKNESS

An ocean over our heads

By the next day, we had already forgotten all our sufferings. At first I was surprised that I didn't feel thirsty, and wondered why. The stream running at my feet provided the answer.

We had breakfast and drank some of the healthy water. I felt very cheerful. Why shouldn't a man as determined as my uncle succeed with his expedition, when he had a guide as hard-working as Hans, and a nephew as loving as myself? If anyone now suggested that I return to the top of Sneffels, I would certainly refuse.

In any case, all we had to do was descend.

We set off again at 8.00 a.m. on Thursday 9th July. The granite passage twisted and turned but the general direction was always south-east. My uncle kept looking at his compass to check.

The slope here was very slight. The stream ran gently beside us, and I thought of it as a friendly goddess guiding us on our way. I was merry — but my uncle wasn't. He cursed the path, which he said was horizontal. His only interest, it seemed to me, was in paths that were vertical.

That day and next, we went a long way along, but only a very little way down.

By the evening of Friday 10th July, we calculated that we were seventy-five miles south-east of Reykjavik, and seven miles deep.

Suddenly, we came to a large, and very frightening hole in the floor of the passage — what geologists call a fault. We stood on the edge of it. My uncle clapped his hands for joy when he saw how steep it was, and how far down it went.

'Now we shall make real progress!' he cried.

Hans fastened the ropes safely around us and the descent continued. I can't say that it seemed dangerous — by now, I was used to this sort of thing.

We went round and round, down a natural staircase that looked man-made. Every quarter of an hour we rested, talking as we ate, and drank from the stream. The Hansbach had turned into a waterfall, and it provided more than enough water for our thirst.

On 11th and 12th July, still following the staircase, we went another five miles into the earth's crust. Now we were about thirteen miles below sea-level.

On 13th July, the way became much easier, sloping gently to the south-east at about forty-five degrees. As there was not much scenery, it also became rather uninteresting.

On Wednesday 15th July, according to the Professor's calculations, we were eighteen miles underground, and about 125 miles from Sneffels. When I heard this, I exclaimed in surprise.

'What are you thinking, my boy?' he asked.

'I was thinking that, if your calculations are correct, we are no longer under Iceland.'

'Is that so?'

'We can easily check.'

I looked at the map and made some measurements.

'I was right,' I said. 'We must have passed Cape Portland and be south-east of Iceland, under the sea.'

'Under the sea,' repeated my uncle, rubbing his hands with delight.

'So the ocean is over our heads!' I exclaimed.

'Why, what could be more natural, Axel? Aren't there coal mines in the north of England that extend under the sea?'

The Professor might consider it natural, but I didn't like the thought of all that water over my head. Still, it didn't make much difference whether it was mountains or sea on top of us, as long as the granite was strong enough to hold everything up. I quickly got used to the idea as the passage led us deeper and deeper to the south-east. Soon we were very far down indeed.

A few days later, on the evening of Saturday 18th July, we arrived in a huge granite hall. My uncle paid Hans his weekly wages. The next day, it was decided, should be a day of rest.

A day of rest

I awoke lazily on Sunday morning. We were now used to our life underground. I scarcely thought about sun, stars and moon, about trees, houses or towns any more. To us, living as cavemen, these things were useless.

Our faithful stream flowed across the floor of the hall. We had travelled so far that its water was now cool enough to drink straight away.

After breakfast, the Professor decided to put his daily notes in order.

'When we get back to Germany,' he said, 'I want to be able to draw a map of our journey underground.'

'That will be very interesting, Uncle, but are your observations exact enough?'

'Yes, I have written down every angle and every slope. So, first let us work out our exact position. Take the compass, and tell me in which direction we've been travelling.'

I studied it.

'East by south,' I replied.

'Good,' said the Professor, making some rapid calculations. 'I estimate that we have travelled 213 miles from our starting point.'

'So we are under the Atlantic Ocean?'
'Exactly.'
'And a storm may be raging above us? And ships may be tossing about on the waves?'
'Yes.'
'And whales may be beating the roof of our prison with their tails?'
'Don't worry, Axel. They won't be able to shake it. Let's think about our position again. We are 213 miles south-east of Sneffels, and I estimate that we are forty-eight miles below the surface.'
'But scientists think that that is the limit of the earth's crust!'
'I know.'
'And, if you're right, the temperature ought to be 1,500°C.'
'Ought to be, my boy.'
'And all this granite ought to be melting.'
'Well, you can see that it is not melting. What does the thermometer say?'
'27.6°C.'
'So the scientists are wrong by 1,472.4 degrees, and Humphry Davy was right. What do you say about that?'
'Nothing.'

I still believed in the theory that the centre of the earth was a ball of fire, and that the further you went down, the hotter you would become. However, I had to agree that we had come a long way down, and I felt no heat myself. Perhaps the lava around the walls simply did not allow the heat to pass through. But I did not bother to argue. I just changed the subject.

'Uncle,' I said, 'at Iceland, the radius of the earth is about 4,800 miles, isn't it?'
'Yes.'
'And we have done forty-eight of those miles.'
'Yes.'
'In about twenty days.'

'Yes, in about twenty days.'

'At that rate, it will take us 2,000 days to reach the centre! Nearly five and a half years!'

The Professor did not reply.

'And anyway, if we travel 213 miles horizontally for every 48 miles vertically, we shall come out at some point on the earth's surface long before we reach the centre!' I added.

'Your calculations must be wrong!' shouted my uncle angrily. 'Another man has done this journey, and I'm going to do it, too.'

'I hope so but … '

'Hold your tongue, Axel, and stop talking nonsense. Just look at the manometer. What does it say?'

'It shows the pressure is quite high.'

'Good. You can see that, by descending gradually, our bodies have got used to breathing this air, and thus we have avoided trouble.'

'Except for slight earache.'

'That's nothing. You can stop it by breathing quickly.'

'Of course,' I replied, determined not to annoy my uncle again. 'It's even a pleasure to live down here. Have you noticed how clearly we can hear?'

'I have.'

'But won't this density increase?'

'It will. The density will increase, and we will get lighter and lighter.'

'Then how shall we continue our descent?'

'We shall have to fill our pockets with stones.'

'You have an answer for everything, Uncle,' I replied doubtfully.

There was one question my uncle would not be able to answer, however. Even if Arne Saknussemm had done this journey, how did he know when he had reached the centre of the earth? The manometer had not been invented at that time, so he would have had no way of knowing exactly how far down he had gone.

But I didn't ask this. We spent the rest of that Sunday in calculations and conversation. I agreed with everything the Professor said, and I wished I had Hans's ability to do what my uncle wanted, without asking any questions.

Lost

Steep slopes now led us deep into the earth. Some days we advanced as much as four or five miles towards the centre. These were very dangerous descents, which we managed to climb down only with Hans's knowledge and strength.

More than two weeks passed. By 7th August, we were seventy-five miles down. We had seventy-five miles of rock, ocean, land and towns over us! We must have been about 500 miles from Iceland.

All through that day, the passage sloped very little. I was in front. My uncle had one lamp and I had the other.

At one point, I stopped to look at some granite. I turned round to ask my uncle a question, and discovered that I was alone.

'Well,' I thought, 'I was walking too fast, or Hans and my uncle have stopped somewhere. I must go back. Luckily, it's an easy climb.'

I walked back for a quarter of an hour, but saw nobody. I called out, but nobody replied. My voice was lost in the echoes.

I began to feel frightened.

'Keep calm,' I said aloud. 'There's only one path. I was in front, so I must go back.'

I climbed for another half an hour. I listened, in case anyone was calling me. In that density, sound travelled a long way. But the passage was strangely silent.

I could not believe I was alone. I could not be lost. And even if I were, people who are lost always find their way again.

'As there's only one path, and the other two are on it,' I said to myself, 'I am certain to find them. All I have to do is keep climbing. Unless, of course, they forgot that I was in front and have turned back, too. But even then I shall catch them if I hurry. Of course I shall.'

I only half-believed my own words. Besides, it took me a long time to put together even these simple ideas.

Then I wondered if I really had been in front. Yes, that was certain. Hans had been following me, ahead of my uncle. He had stopped to fasten his pack on his shoulders. I must have gone ahead at that moment.

'Oh, in any case,' I remembered, 'there is my faithful stream. All I need to do is follow it back up, and I shall find my companions.'

The thought cheered me up. How wise of my uncle to prevent Hans from stopping up the hole in the wall! Having supplied us with water for weeks, the stream would now be my guide, too. I bent to wash in the Hansbach before continuing my climb.

To my horror, I found that I was standing on rough, dry granite. The stream was no longer flowing at my feet!

To describe my despair at that moment is impossible. I was buried alive. I thought then that I would die of hunger and thirst.

My hands passed over the granite floor. How hard and dry the rock seemed!

Now I knew the reason for that strange silence when I had listened for my companions' voices. But how had I lost the stream? Clearly, the passage had divided and I had taken one route, while the Hansbach and my companions had taken the other.

I was lost! Lost beneath seventy-five miles of rock!

I tried to think about things on the surface — about Hamburg, the house on King's Street and my poor little Grauben; about our journey to Iceland, Mr Fridriksson and Sneffels. But what human power could open the rock above me, and take me back there? Who could even show me the way back to my companions?

'Oh, Uncle!' I exclaimed in despair.

I thought of asking heaven for help. Memories of when I was a child came back. I knelt in prayer.

This calmed me slightly, and I was able to think about my situation.

My water-bottle was full, and I had enough food for three days. Should I go up or down? Up, of course, until I reached the point where I had left the stream. Then, with the stream at my feet, I still might be able to get back to the top of Sneffels.

Why hadn't I thought of that before? Here was a chance of reaching safety. I must find the Hansbach again.

I started walking. The slope was rather steep, but I felt hopeful, knowing that I had no choice. Then, after half an hour, the path came to an end. I bumped into a wall of solid rock, and fell to the ground.

I lay there in terror and despair, my last hope gone. I would never get out. I would die the most dreadful of deaths. I tried to speak aloud but no sound came. I could scarcely breathe.

Then I noticed a new horror. My lamp had broken when I fell, and was gradually going out. I watched its light slowly fading away. Shadows passed along the walls. The precious light was going, going … Finally it went out altogether, and I was in total darkness.

A terrible cry burst from my lips. No light! I was blind! I stood up, with my arms stretched out in front of me, trying to feel my way. I started to rush downwards, downwards all the time, crying, shouting, hurting myself on the sharp rocks, falling, getting up again, trying to drink the blood that was running down my face.

I shall never know where I ran. After several hours, I fainted, and fell to the ground.

THE LIDENBROCK SEA

Voices

When I became conscious again, my face was wet with tears. I had no way of knowing how long I had been unconscious. No man had ever been so alone. I was covered with blood from my fall. I did not want to think any more. In pain, wishing I were already dead, I rolled across the floor to the opposite wall.

Then I heard a loud noise, like thunder, which gradually faded away. Where could it have come from? Perhaps from an underground explosion.

I listened, in case it happened again. A quarter of an hour passed in complete silence. Suddenly my ear, which happened to be against the wall, heard words. They were far away, but they were words.

For a moment I was afraid that the words might be my own, brought back by an echo. Perhaps I had cried out without knowing. I closed my lips tightly and put my ear against the wall again.

Yes, someone was speaking. Even when I dragged myself a few feet further along the wall, I could hear it. I was sure I heard a sad voice repeat the word 'lost'.

Who was speaking? Clearly, it was either my uncle or Hans. No one else was down here. And if I could hear them, they must be able to hear me.

'Help!' I cried as loudly as I could. 'Help!'

I listened for some reply. None came. The word 'lost' reached me again, followed by the same sound like thunder. Then I heard my name. I had heard my uncle talking!

Suddenly I understood. The sounds weren't coming through the wall — they couldn't, it was solid granite — but they were coming along the wall.

I had to hurry, in case my uncle moved away from the wall. If he did, he would not be able to hear me. I put my mouth close to the wall and, as clearly as possible, said, 'Uncle Lidenbrock!'

For some time — it seemed like centuries — there was complete silence. At last these words reached me: 'Axel! Axel! Is that you?'

'Yes, yes!' I replied.

For almost a minute I heard nothing else. Then my uncle's voice again seemed to come from the granite wall.

'Where are you, Axel?'

'Lost, in complete darkness.'

Once more, there was a long pause.

'But what about your lamp?'

'Gone out.'

There was a pause.

'And the stream?'

'Disappeared.'

Pause.

'Axel, my poor boy, cheer up!'

'I'm exhausted. You talk.'

I thought that when he was not talking to me, my uncle was probably talking to Hans, and that I couldn't hear him then. But these pauses were very strange. They all seemed to be about the same length.

'Have courage,' my uncle called. 'We've been up and down the passage looking for you, in vain. Finally, we came back down the Hansbach, firing our guns. Well, don't despair, Axel. At least now we can hear each other.'

Already, faint hope had returned to me. I put my lips close to the wall.

'Uncle!' I said.

'Yes, my boy,' came the reply about thirty seconds later.

'I think we are quite a long way apart. We must find out how far it is. Do you have your chronometer?'

Another half minute.

'Yes.'

'Then say my name, noticing the exact second at which you speak. As soon as I hear it, I'll repeat my name,

The Lidenbrock Sea

and you must notice the second at which my reply reaches you.'

Pause.

'Right. Are you ready?'

'Yes.'

Pause.

'I'm going to say your name now.'

As soon as I heard Axel, I replied Axel. Then I waited.

'Forty seconds,' said my uncle. 'There were forty seconds between the time I said Axel and the time I heard you say it. So sound takes twenty seconds to travel between us. At 1,020 feet a second, that makes 20,400 feet, or just under four miles.'

'Four miles!' I muttered to myself, and then called to my uncle, 'Should I go up or down?'

Pause.

'Down, and I'll tell you why. We are in a huge cave with many passages leading into it. The one you are in is sure to lead here because all the cracks and gaps seem to start from this place. So get up and start walking. Drag yourself along if you have to. Slide down the steep slopes, and our arms will be ready to welcome you at the end. Come, my boy, come!'

His words encouraged me.

'I'm leaving now, Uncle,' I cried. 'We won't be able to talk once I've left here, so goodbye!'

I waited. 'Goodbye, Axel, goodbye!'

Those words completed our conversation. Amazingly we had been talking to one another through the earth, over a distance of nearly four miles. I realized that, as I could hear my uncle, nothing could be between us. If I followed the sound, I would reach him.

I got up, dragging myself along. The slope was quite steep, and I let myself slide. I went faster and faster. I no longer had the strength to stop myself. Then the ground disappeared from under my feet, and I felt myself falling straight down. My head hit a rock and I lost consciousness.

Saved

When I became conscious again, I was lying on blankets in half-darkness. My uncle held my hand at my first sigh. When I opened my eyes, he gave a cry of joy.

'My dear boy,' said my uncle, taking me in his arms, 'you are saved!'

I was overcome by his words and actions. Such tenderness from the Professor was rare.

He told me that I had been alone for three days. I was very weak, so I let myself go to sleep again, thinking about it.

Next morning, when I woke up, I looked around. My bed, made up of all our blankets, was in a delightful cave, with stalactites and a soft carpet of fine sand. No lamps were burning, but there was light coming in through a narrow opening. I could also hear a mysterious noise like waves on a shore, and then a sound like the wind.

Was I dreaming? Or had my head been cracked in my fall?

'No, that really is daylight,' I thought, 'slipping in between the rocks. That really is the noise of waves, and the whistling of the wind. Have we returned to the surface then? Has my uncle given up the expedition, or has he finished it successfully?'

The Professor appeared. He asked me how I was, and I told him that apart from being very hungry, I felt very well. I also added that I thought the fall must have damaged my brain.

'Your brain?' My uncle seemed quite surprised.

'Yes. We haven't returned to the surface, have we?'

'No, certainly not.'

'Then I must be mad. I can see daylight, and I can hear the wind and the sea.'

'Oh, is that all?'

'Won't you explain?'

'You shall see it with your own eyes.'

'Then let's go out!' I cried, sitting up.
'No, Axel. The open air might be bad for you.'
'The open air?'
'Yes, the wind is rather strong.'
'But I feel perfectly well.'
'Have a little patience, my boy. Our voyage may be a long one.'
'Voyage?'
'Yes. Rest today, and tomorrow we'll set sail.'

Set sail? Was there a river or a lake out there? Was a ship waiting for us in some underground harbour? My curiosity was so violent that my uncle decided it would be better to let me go outside and see.

I dressed quickly, wrapped one of the blankets around me and left the cave.

Amazing wonders

At first, I saw nothing. My eyes were not used to the light now, and they closed immediately. When I was able to open them again, I was more surprised than delighted.

'The sea!' I cried.

'The Lidenbrock Sea,' said my uncle. 'I found it, so I have a right to call it by my name!'

Water, the beginning of a lake or an ocean, stretched away out of sight. There was a sloping beach of fine, golden sand, covered with small shells. Waves echoed strangely as they broke on it. A wind blew some of the water in my face. Behind the beach, a line of cliffs curved up to great heights.

It was a real sea, but empty and wild in appearance.

And the light that showed it to me was neither warm and brilliant like that of the sun, nor cold and pale like that of the moon. It was a strong, cool, white light, that was clearly electric.

Over my head, instead of a sky shining with stars, there were huge clouds. The effect was sad. Above those clouds, I knew, there was a granite roof.

We were indeed still in a cave, although the word gives no idea of the size of it. The shore, like the water, stretched out of sight, and the clouds, I estimated, were 12,000 feet high.

I did not know what theory could explain such a place. No cave known to man compared with this one, with its cloudy sky, electric light, and huge sea. I looked at it in silence. New words were needed for such sights, and I could not produce them. I looked, I thought, I admired — with amazement mixed with fear.

But my uncle had stopped being amazed at such wonders.

'Do you feel strong enough to walk about a little?' he asked me.

'Yes,' I replied. It was wonderful to breathe that wet, salty air after forty days below ground.

'Then hold my arm, and let us go along the shore.'

On the left, steep rocks were piled on top of each other. Water poured down their sides. Streams flowed gently into the sea, among them our faithful Hansbach.

'We shall miss it in the future,' I said with a sigh.

'Nonsense!' said the Professor ungratefully. 'What does it matter which stream is with us?'

Five hundred yards away, a strange forest appeared. Its trees looked like open umbrellas, and the wind did not move them at all. It was as if they were made of stone.

I walked faster, anxious to find out what trees they were. When we arrived under their shade, my surprise turned to excitement.

'It's just a forest of mushrooms,' said my uncle.

He was right, but what mushrooms! These were white mushrooms thirty or forty feet high, with heads just as wide. And there were thousands of them, crowded so tightly that no light could get between.

We wandered futher.

'Magnificent, splendid!' cried my uncle. 'Look, Axel, at the bones you are walking on, too.'

'Bones?' I exclaimed. 'Yes, yes! These are the bones of huge prehistoric animals.'

I picked one up.

'Here is the lower jaw of one,' I said, 'and over there is the leg bone of another. Animals have lived on the shores of this underground sea, in the shade of these giant plants. I can even see some complete skeletons.'

I had a thought. Some of the monsters might still be alive, wandering in the cold forests, or behind the steep rocks. I looked carefully around me in some alarm, but I could see nothing. We were the only living creatures in this underground world.

After another hour, we returned along the beach to the cave, where I fell into a deep sleep.

The raft

I awoke the next day feeling completely cured. I swam in the sea for a few minutes, thinking it would do me good, and came back hungry for breakfast.

Hans was the cook, and as he now had both fire and water, he could do more interesting dishes than usual. He even served coffee. Never had that drink tasted so wonderful!

'Now,' said my uncle, 'the tide is rising and we must study it.'

'The tide?' I exclaimed.

'Yes, of course.'

'You mean that the influence of the moon and sun extends down here?'

'Why not?'

At that moment, we were walking on the sandy beach and, yes, the waves were gradually moving closer to us.

'You are right!' I cried. 'I can scarcely believe my eyes. I should never have thought that deep down inside the earth there would be a real ocean with tides, winds and storms.'

'Why not?' said my uncle again. 'Is there any scientific reason against it?'

'None that I know — if we abandon the theory that the centre of the earth is very hot.'

'Then Humphry Davy is right?'

'Clearly. So there may be other seas like this one. And they may contain fish! Let's make some lines and hooks!'

'We will, Axel. We must discover all we can about these new regions.'

'But where exactly are we, Uncle? I haven't asked you that yet.'

'Horizontally, we are 875 miles from Iceland.'

'As far as that? Does the compass still show our direction as south-east?'

'Yes.'

'And how far down are we?'

'Eighty-eight miles.'

'So,' I said, 'the snow-covered mountains of Scotland are above us?'

'Yes,' laughed the Professor. 'It's rather a heavy weight to support, but the ceiling is solid. It's built of the best material!'

'Oh, I'm not afraid of the roof falling in,' I said. 'But now, Uncle, what are your plans?'

'We shall indeed continue our journey downwards, as everything has been so successful so far.'

'But how can we get below all this water?'

'I'm not going to dive in head first! I'm sure we shall find new openings on the opposite shore.'

'And how far do you think that is?'

THE LIDENBROCK SEA

'Between seventy and a hundred miles.'

'Ah!' I said, thinking to myself that this estimate could be quite wrong.

'So we mustn't waste time, we must set sail tomorrow.'

'All right,' I said, 'but where's the boat?'

'Not a boat, my boy. We shall make a good, solid raft.'

'A raft?' I cried. 'But a raft is as hard to build as a boat, and I don't see ... '

'You don't see, Axel, but if you listened you might hear.'

'Hear?'

'Yes, hear some hammering. Hans is already building our raft. Come and see.'

After walking for quarter of an hour, we found Hans at work in a small natural harbour behind a cliff. To my surprise, a half-finished raft was lying on the sand. It was made from beams of a strange kind of wood, and there was a lot more wood like it lying all around.

'What wood is this, Uncle?'

'It's fossil wood, my boy, wood that has been turned to mineral by the action of the sea water.'

'But then surely it must be as hard as stone and too heavy to float?'

'Not the pieces that are only partly fossilized. Look,' added my uncle, throwing one such piece into the water.

It disappeared from sight. Then it rose again to the surface, and floated on the waves.

'Amazing!' I cried.

Next evening, the raft was finished. It was ten feet long and five feet wide. Its wooden beams were bound with strong ropes to form a solid deck. Its mast was two long poles tied together, its sail was one of our blankets. We pushed it into the water, and it floated peacefully on the Lidenbrock Sea.

8

THE VOYAGE

Prehistoric day-dreams

On 13th August we awoke early, eager to travel this new and easy way.

Everything was loaded on board — food, instruments, tools, fire-arms, a large supply of fresh water. At six o'clock, the Professor told us to get on board, too.

Hans was steering. I let go of the rope that held us to the shore, and we moved out.

As we were leaving the little harbour, my uncle suggested we should give it a name.

'Grauben,' I suggested. 'Port Grauben would look very nice on your map.'

'Port Grauben it shall be,' agreed my uncle.

The wind was blowing from the north-west. We sailed with it, at great speed.

'If we go on at this rate,' said my uncle after an hour, 'we shall travel at least seventy-five miles in twenty-four hours, and it won't be long before we reach the other shore.'

I did not reply, but went and sat at the front, watching. Soon we were completely out of sight of land.

At about midday, huge pieces of seaweed came floating past. I knew that seaweed could be big enough to stop a ship but none, surely, could be as big as that seaweed on the Lidenbrock Sea. Some pieces were 4,000 feet long! What natural elements could produce such gigantic plants?

Evening came but it did not get dark. The light over this sea was constant. After supper, I stretched out by the mast, and fell into a pleasant sleep.

The next day, as my uncle had instructed, I started to keep a diary of our strange voyage.

Friday 14th August

Steady north-west wind. Raft sailing fast and straight. Seventy-five miles from Port Grauben. Nothing on the horizon. Same constant light. Weather fine. Temperature 32°C.

At midday, Hans fastened a hook and bit of meat on to the end of a line, and threw it over the side. For two hours he caught nothing. We began to think the waters were uninhabited. Then the line tightened, and Hans pulled in a struggling fish.

We examined the creature carefully. In some ways it was like a sturgeon — a large fish that lives in the rivers of Russia, and yet it was different. It had, for example, no teeth or tail.

The Professor decided it belonged to an extinct family of fish, now known only as fossils.

'What!' I cried. 'You mean we've caught an extinct fish, alive?'

'Yes,' replied the Professor continuing to look at it, 'and you'll notice something strange about it — something peculiar, so they say, to fish in underground waters.'

'What's that?'

'It's blind.'

'Blind?'

'Not only blind. It has no eyes at all.'

I looked at the fish. What my uncle said was true. But as this creature might be an exception, we threw the line over the side again. In two hours we caught many fish belonging to extinct families. None of them had eyes.

I looked up in the air. As there were extinct fish around, why should there not also be extinct birds, feeding on them?

My imagination carried me away, and I had a prehistoric day-dream — first of great animals, then of enormous birds, then of the reptiles that came before them, and of the fish before them.

Further and further back I dreamed, of the time before animals, when plants were the only things that lived in the great heat. Then I dreamed of the time before plants, when there was no rock at all, and the earth was nothing but gas, white-hot and as big and bright as the sun.

What a dream! As if in a fever, I wrote it all down. I thought of nothing else — the Professor, our guide, or even the raft.

'What's the matter?' asked my uncle.

I stared at him without seeing him.

'Be careful, Axel!'

I felt Hans seize me. If he hadn't, I might have fallen off the raft and into the sea.

'Has he gone mad?' cried the Professor.

'What is it?' I said at last.

'Are you ill?'

'No, no, I was dreaming. It's over now ... Is everything all right?'

'Yes, there's a good wind and a fine sea. We should see land soon.'

I stood and looked at the horizon. There was still nothing to see except water and clouds.

Saturday 15th August

No land in sight.

My uncle was in a bad temper. Now that I had recovered, his old impatience had returned.

'You seem anxious, Uncle,' I said, seeing him study the horizon through his telescope again and again.

'Anxious? Not at all!'

'Impatient, then.'
'Yes, for a good reason.'
'But we are moving very fast.'
'What use is that? This sea is too big!'

I remembered that the Professor had estimated his Lidenbrock Sea was about seventy-five miles across. We had sailed three times that far but there was still no sign of the south shore.

'And we aren't going down,' the Professor continued. 'It's a waste of time. I didn't come on this trip just to sail on a pond!'

He called this journey a trip, this sea a pond!

'But,' I said, 'as we're following the route taken by Saknussemm ... '

'Well, that's another problem' said my uncle. 'I am beginning to wonder if Saknussemm really did come to this sea. Did he cross it? Did that stream lead us to the right place?'

'Anyhow, the views are magnificent and ... '

'I don't care about views! I've decided to do something and I'm going to do it.'

I left the Professor alone with his impatience. At six in the evening Hans asked for his wages, and the money was counted out.

Sunday 16th August

Nothing new. The same weather. The same electric light. A slightly fresher wind. This sea seems to go on for ever. It must be as big as the Mediterranean, or even the Atlantic.

My uncle tied one of our heaviest axes to the end of a rope which he let down 1,200 feet. There was no bottom. It was difficult to pull the axe up again. When it was back on board, Hans showed me some deep marks in it. I looked at him.

'Teeth,' he said, opening and shutting his mouth several times to help me understand.

'Teeth!' I said in amazement, looking more closely. Yes, those were definitely the marks of teeth on metal. The jaws that contained them must be powerful indeed. Did they belong to some prehistoric monster that lived deep beneath the surface? A monster more terrible than a shark or a whale? Was my day-dream going to come true? I could not forget the idea.

The battle of the sea-monsters

Monday 17th August

All day I thought of those teeth-marks, and the sort of reptile that might have made them. Was I going to meet a prehistoric monster? I watched the sea in terror. Professor Lidenbrock seemed to have had the same idea, if not the same fear for, after examining the axe, he kept looking closely at the ocean.

'Why did he let that axe down?' I said to myself. 'It has disturbed some creature and we may be attacked.'

I looked at our guns to make sure they would work.

Already, from the way the water was moving, I could see that something was happening below us. Danger was near. We must keep watch.

Tuesday 18th August

Evening came, although, with this constant light, we only knew because we felt tired. Hans was steering and, as everything was quiet and calm, I fell asleep.

Two hours later, I was woken up violently. The raft had been lifted above the water, and thrown a hundred feet or more.

'What's the matter?' cried my uncle. 'Have we hit land?'

Hans pointed to a dark shape rising and falling a quarter of a mile away.

'It's a giant porpoise!' I cried.

'Yes,' said my uncle, 'and there is a giant sea-lizard.'

A moment later the sea-lizard went under the waves. Then we saw something else.

'Look! Over there! A huge crocodile! Look at its rows of teeth! Oh, it's disappearing.'

'A whale! A whale!' cried the Professor. 'See how large it is!' At that moment a great spout of air and water shot up from the animal.

We stood there looking in surprise and horror at these sea-monsters. The smallest of them could have broken our raft with one bite of its jaws. Hans wanted to turn around, but in the other direction he saw creatures just as frightening — a turtle forty feet long, and a serpent thirty feet long, its enormous neck stretched high above the waves, and its head turning this way and that.

Escape was impossible. The reptiles came closer and closer to the raft. I picked up my rifle, but what effect could that have on such creatures?

We were dumb with fright. The crocodile and the serpent came still closer. The rest had disappeared. I got ready to fire, but Hans stopped me. The two monsters passed within a hundred yards of the raft — and threw themselves at each other without noticing us.

The battle began 200 yards away. We could see the two monsters gripping each other. Then I thought that the other animals had come back to join in. I pointed all six of the reptiles out to the Icelander, but he shook his head.

'There are only two,' he said.

'He's right,' said my uncle, who had the telescope.

'He can't be!' I cried.

'Yes, he is. The first of those monsters has the nose of a porpoise,

the head of a lizard and the teeth of a crocodile. It's the most fearful of prehistoric reptiles, the ichthyosaurus!'

'And the other?'

'The other is the enemy of the first — a serpent with a turtle's shell, the plesiosaurus!'

Hans was right. Only two monsters were disturbing the surface of the sea — an ichthyosaurus at least a hundred feet long, with eyes as big as a man's head, and a plesiosaurus with a neck that rose thirty feet above the water.

These two attacked each other with an anger impossible to describe. They made mountainous waves that nearly turned us over. They made a terrible noise as they fought. They were so close that we could not see where one monster began and the other ended.

One hour, two hours passed. The fight in all its violence continued. We stood without moving, ready to shoot. Suddenly both monsters disappeared beneath the water. Was the fight going to finish in the depths of the sea?

Several minutes passed. Then an enormous head shot out of the water, the head of the plesiosaurus. The monster was dying. I could no longer see its shell, but its long neck was rising and falling. The water flew all around and almost blinded us. But soon the movements became less violent, and the body of the serpent lay stretched out on the calm waves.

Wednesday 19th August

Luckily the wind is blowing hard, so we have been able to get quickly away from the scene of the battle. Hans is still steering. My uncle has become even more impatient, and looks anxiously at the horizon all the time.

The island

Thursday 20th August

Wind north-north-east. Temperature high. Speed about ten miles per hour.

The Voyage

At about midday, we heard a continuous roaring noise in the distance. Hans climbed to the top of the mast but could see nothing.

Three hours passed. The roar seemed to be that of a waterfall. I said so to my uncle, who shook his head. There was definitely something very noisy out there, quite a few miles away. Was it in the sky or the sea? They both looked calm.

At about four o'clock, Hans climbed the mast again. His eyes looked to the horizon and stopped at a certain point.

'He has seen something,' said my uncle.

'Yes, I believe he has.'

Hans came down and pointed to the south.

'Over there,' he said.

My uncle seized his telescope. 'Yes, yes!' he cried.

'What can you see?'

'A huge column of water rising above the waves.'

'Another sea-monster?'

'Perhaps.'

'Then let us steer more to the west.' I said. 'We know how dangerous these monsters are.'

'Straight ahead,' replied my uncle.

I turned to Hans but he steered on.

The nearer we got to the column, the taller it seemed. What creature could take in so much water and shoot it out for so long without stopping? At eight o'clock in the evening, we were less than five miles from the monster. Its huge dark body lay in the sea without moving. It seemed to me to be over a mile long.

The column of water was being thrown 500 feet in the air, and roaring down like rain.

We were rushing towards a powerful monster that would surely be able to eat a hundred whales every day! Terror seized me.

Suddenly, Hans pointed at the object and said, 'Island.'

'An island?' I asked doubtfully.

'Why, yes!' replied the Professor, shaking with laughter.

'But what about that column of water?'

'Geyser,' said Hans.

'Yes, it must be,' agreed my uncle, 'a geyser, like those in Iceland.'

At first, I refused to believe that I could mistake an island for a monster. But the proof was in front of me, and finally I had to admit it.

The island looked just like a whale with its head sixty feet above the water. Now and then we heard explosions, and the enormous column of water shot up to the clouds. The rays of electric light mixed with it to produce many different colours.

'Let us land,' said the Professor.

Hans skilfully steered the raft up to the island. I jumped on to the rocks, and my uncle followed lightly. Hans stayed on board, without curiosity.

The ground was trembling under our feet. I put the thermometer into the boiling water, from which the geyser rose. It showed a temperature of 163°C.

This water was coming from a blazing furnace. There was central heat!

I pointed this out to Professor Lidenbrock.

'We shall see.' That was all he would say.

After naming the island Axel, he led the way back to the raft. Hans had made everything on the raft tidy during our absence, and now we set sail again.

We have now sailed 675 miles from Port Grauben, and are 1,500 miles from Iceland. England is above us.

9

ELECTRIC FIRE

Bad weather

Friday 21st August

The magnificent geyser disappeared behind us, because the wind was stronger, so it had blown us rapidly away from Axel Island.

The weather (if I may use that word) was changing. The air felt heavy, and full of electricity. Gradually the clouds in the south swelled up, and grouped together, getting darker all the time.

There was so much electricity around that my hair stood on end. I felt as if my companions would receive a violent shock if they touched me. On the tops of the mast poles, and on everything else that ended in a point, glowed St Elmo's fire — that strange, electric flame that does not burn.

At ten o'clock in the morning, I had to say it. 'There's bad weather on the way.'

The Professor did not answer. He was in a dreadful temper at the sight of the ocean stretching on and on.

'We're going to have a storm,' I said.

Then there was silence. The wind dropped completely. The raft no longer moved on the sea. Why did we keep the sail up, if a storm was coming?

'Let us take in the sail and remove the mast,' I said. 'That would be sensible.'

'No, a hundred times no!' shouted my uncle. 'Let the wind seize us! Let the storm carry us away! Providing it carries us on to some shore, I don't care if it smashes the raft to pieces.'

He had scarcely said this when there was a change on the southern horizon. Suddenly, the wind blew with the force of a hurricane. It became really dark.

The raft rose into the air and leapt forward, throwing my uncle on to the deck. Hans did not move. His long red hair was being blown forward by the wind. His appearance was terrifying, for from the tip of every hair came little electric flames.

The raft flew along at a speed I could not calculate. The mast stayed firm, although the sail swelled out like a bubble that would burst at any minute.

'The sail! The sail!' I cried, wanting to take it in.

'No!' said my uncle.

'No,' shouted Hans, gently shaking his head.

Now the rain roared down. The curtain of cloud was torn apart, the sea boiled. Brilliant flashes of lightning were followed by great rolls of thunder. Electric flames came from the tops of the waves, so that each one looked like a small volcano.

The lightning flashes were so bright that I could hardly see. I could hardly hear because the thunder was so loud. I had to hold on to the mast, which bent in the storm.

[Here, my notes became very short but they give a better idea of what it was like than my memory could.]

Sunday 23rd August

Where are we? We have been carried along at enormous speed. Last night was dreadful and the storm is still just as strong. The lightning is flashing all the time. Where are we going? My uncle is stretched out at one end of the raft.

It is getting hotter. The thermometer says … [I can't read what I wrote.]

Monday 24th August

Will this never end? My uncle and I are exhausted. Hans is the same as ever. The raft is still going south-east. We are over 500 miles from Axel Island.

At midday, the storm grew even worse. We had to tie ourselves down. The waves went over our heads.

We had not been able to exchange a word for three days. I think I heard my uncle say 'We are finished', but I am not sure.

'Let us take in the sail,' I wrote down for him to read. He moved his head in agreement.

Shipwrecked

At that moment, before I could do anything, a ball of fire appeared on the raft itself, and the mast and sail disappeared. A moment later I saw them high up in the sky, looking like a prehistoric bird.

Half white, half blue, the fire-ball moved over the deck from one object to another. It went near Hans, who simply stared at it. It went near my uncle, who fell on his knees to avoid it. It came near me, pale and trembling before its heat. It danced around one of my feet, which I tried in vain to pull away.

A smell of gas filled the air. Why couldn't I move my foot? Was it fastened to the deck? I realized that the fire-ball had magnetized all the iron on board — the instruments, tools and guns were moving about and sticking to each other. The nails of my boots were stuck to an iron plate in the deck.

At last, with a violent effort, I pulled my foot away just as the ball was going to seize it, and carry me away, too.

Suddenly there was a blaze of light. The ball burst, and we were covered with tongues of fire.

Then everything went dark. I just had time to see my uncle lying on the deck, and Hans was still steering, but small flames were shooting out of him in all directions, because of the electricity.

Tuesday 25th August

I have just returned to consciousness. The storm is still raging. Enormous forks of lightning are flashing about, like serpents in the sky. We are still at sea, and moving at great speed. We must have passed under England, under the Channel, under France, perhaps under the whole of Europe. But I can hear a new noise! Surely it is the sound of the sea breaking upon rocks …

Here ends my diary, which was saved from the wreck.

I cannot say what happened when the raft was thrown on to the rocks. I fell into the sea, and Hans's strong arms saved me from death.

The brave Icelander carried me to a beach where, later, I found myself lying next to my uncle. Then Hans returned to the rocks to save what he could from the wreck.

I could not speak for a whole hour, I was so exhausted. Hans prepared some food, which I could not even touch. I slept, painfully.

Next day, the weather was excellent. I was woken up by the Professor's cheerful voice.

'Well, my boy, have you slept well?'

'I still feel tired,' I replied, 'but you seem very cheerful, Uncle.'

'I'm delighted, my boy, delighted! We've arrived.'

'At the end of our expedition?'

'No, but at the end of the sea that seemed to go on for ever. Now we can travel by land again and really go down.'

'Uncle, may I ask you a question?'

'You may, Axel, you may.'

'What about our return journey?'

Electric Fire

'Very simple. We shall either find some new route or go back the way we came. I don't imagine it will close behind us.'

'Then we must repair the raft.'

'Of course.'

'But have we enough food to continue?'

'Oh, Hans is very clever, I'm sure he saved most of it. Let us go and see.'

I thought everything must have been destroyed in the wreck, but I was wrong. We found Hans on the shore with our things neatly arranged around him. My uncle was very thankful when he saw how much had been saved, and shook his hand. While we had been lying asleep on the beach, the Icelander had risked his life to save our possessions. Our guns had been lost, but everything else seemed to be there, including the gunpowder and all the instruments.

'Here is the manometer,' exclaimed the Professor, 'the most useful instrument of all, the one which will tell me when we reach the centre. Without it, we might go too far!'

His cheerfulness was frightening.

'But where's the compass?' I asked.

'Here on this rock, with the chronometer and the thermometer. Hans is splendid!'

'What about the food?' I asked.

'Let us see,' replied the Professor.

The boxes which contained our food were laid out in a row. Biscuits, salt meat, gin, dried fish ... We had enough for another four months.

'Four months!' cried the Professor. 'We have time to get to the centre and back. With what remains, I shall give a dinner to the other professors at the Johannaeum!'

I ought to have been used to my uncle by now, but the man still amazed me.

'Now,' he said, 'we must fill our bottles with the rain-water the storm has left in these rocks. And I shall ask

Hans to repair the raft, although I don't think we shall need it again.'

'Why not?' I cried.

'Just an idea, my boy. I don't think we shall leave by the way we came in.'

He didn't know then how right he was.

'Let's go and have breakfast,' he said.

I followed him after he had given instructions to Hans. During the meal — which was one of the best I have ever tasted — I asked the Professor where he thought we were.

'It's certainly difficult to say exactly,' he answered. 'I've not been able to keep a record for the last three days. Still, I can make an estimate.'

'Well, at the island with the geyser ...'

'Axel Island, my boy, the first island to be discovered under the earth.'

'All right, at Axel Island we had travelled across 675 miles of the Lidenbrock Sea, and we were over 1,500 miles from Iceland.'

'Good. Let us start from that point. There were about four days of storm during which we must have travelled at least 200 miles every twenty-four hours.'

'That adds up to 800 miles.'

'Yes, and it means that the Lidenbrock Sea is about 1,500 miles from shore to shore. Do you realize, Axel, it is as wide as the Mediterranean?'

'What is more,' I said, 'if our calculations are correct, the Mediterranean itself is over our heads!'

'Really?'

'Yes, because we are 2,250 miles from Reykjavik.'

'That is a long way my boy, but we can't be sure we are under the Mediterranean unless we are sure our direction did not change during the storm.'

'I'm certain it didn't. The wind seemed to stay the same. I think this shore is south-east of Port Grauben.'

'Well, we can easily find out by looking at the direction on the compass.'

The Professor led the way back to the rock on which Hans had placed the instruments. He picked up the compass and looked at the needle. He rubbed his eyes and looked again. Then he turned to me in amazement.

'What's the matter?' I asked.

He told me to look at the instrument. I exclaimed in surprise. The north tip of the needle was pointing to what we thought was south! It was pointing towards the land instead of out to sea!

I shook the compass and examined it carefully. It was working perfectly. But wherever I put it, the needle showed this unexpected direction. During the storm, the wind must have changed and brought the raft back to the shore we thought we had left behind.

A human head

I have never seen a man so surprised at first, and so angry afterwards. All those days and dangers to be repeated!

'So air, fire and water have combined to stop me, have they?' he shouted. 'Well, they'll see how strong I am! I won't give up! We shall see whether Man or Nature will win!'

I tried to calm him. 'Listen to me,' I said firmly. 'We can't do the impossible. Nobody can sail against the wind for a thousand miles on a collection of rotten beams with a blanket for a sail and two sticks for a mast. We would be mad to try it again ... '

I was able to continue like this for ten minutes, simply because the Professor was not listening to a word I said.

'To the raft!' he cried. That was his only reply. It was no use arguing. His will was harder than granite.

Hans had just finished repairing the raft, as if he had guessed. He put all our things on board. The sky was clear, the wind was blowing steadily from the north-west.

What could I do against the two of them, against such a master and such a servant? I was about to step on board when my uncle stopped me.

'We won't leave until tomorrow,' he said. 'We must explore this part of the coast now that we are here.'

If we had returned to the north shore, you understand, we had not returned to Port Grauben. That, we decided, was further west. So it was sensible to look around this new region.

'Let's start exploring, then,' I said.

Hans stayed with the raft while the Professor and I set off. The space between the sea and the cliffs was very wide at this point. Near the cliffs, we walked over huge shells, in which prehistoric creatures had lived, and over stones washed smooth by the sea, although no water had reached them for thousands of years.

'Ah!' I said to myself, 'this partly explains the existence of the Lidenbrock Sea. Our seas on the surface flowed down here through some crack, and now the water has evaporated a little because of the heat. This is the reason for the clouds and all the electricity.'

I was satisfied with this theory. The wonders of Nature can always be explained by physical laws, I thought.

We had walked for about a mile when the ground changed. It became very rough, full of hollows. We were advancing over it with difficulty, when suddenly we came upon a plain piled high with bones. Row after row of them stretched away to the horizon. There, before us, the whole history of animal life was laid out!

We rushed forward, our feet cracking and crushing the fossils and bones that museums fight about.

I was so surprised I could not say anything. My uncle lifted his arms towards the clouds, his mouth open, his eyes flashing at the sight of this collection beyond price.

A few minutes later, he picked up a skull.

'Axel! Look, Axel!' he cried, in a voice trembling with excitement. 'A human head.'

To understand my uncle's excitement at finding a skull, you need to know what had happened in Europe just before we left.

In 1863, near Abbeville in France, a human jaw-bone had been found with some stone axes. It was the first human fossil of this sort that had ever been discovered.

Many scientists, including Professor Lidenbrock, believed that it belonged to the Quaternary Period. Others did not believe it was so early. There were long arguments between the two sides.

So you will realize my uncle's joy when he found first a head, and then a complete body, of Quaternary Man!

I stood in silent wonder. My uncle, who usually talked so much, was also silent. We lifted the body and leaned it against a rock. It looked back at us out of the hollows of its eyes.

Then my uncle became the Professor once more. He seized the skeleton and held it up.

'You can see that this is a human fossil, about six feet tall, of the Caucasian race. How he got here, I do not know. Perhaps in the Quaternary Period, parts of the earth's surface slipped down through gaps in the earth's crust. It does not matter. Unless he came here recently, like myself, as a tourist, then he must be Quaternary Man!'

The Professor finished and I clapped loudly. My uncle was quite right, and we found more skeletons at every step to prove it.

But then we thought of something alarming. Were these men already dead when they fell down to the shores of the Lidenbrock Sea? Or had they lived here, in this underground world under this false sky? So far we had seen only fish and sea-monsters. Might human beings also be down here still, living in the same way as they had lived thousands of years ago?

10
THE TUNNEL

A dagger on the sea-shore

We walked on over the piles of bones we had discovered, driven by our burning curiosity. What other wonders might this place contain? What new treasures might we discover for science?

After another mile, we reached the edge of a huge forest. The tall trees and plants were brown and faded-looking, from the lack of sun. The leaves had no colour, and the flowers had no scent. The forest looked almost as if it were made of paper.

My uncle went straight in and, hesitating slightly, I followed him. As there was so much vegetation, might we not meet more monsters?

Suddenly I stopped, holding my uncle back. I thought I saw some enormous animals, not fossils this time, but living creatures. Yes, yes! I saw mastodons — gigantic elephants that had not been seen on earth for more than 10,000 years, tearing at the trees, and eating the branches. So that dream I had had of the prehistoric world was coming true! And we were unprotected!

My uncle looked, and looked again.

'Forward!' he said, seizing my arm.

'No!' I cried. 'No! We have no weapons. No human could walk safely among those monsters.'

'No human?' asked my uncle, more quietly. 'You are wrong, Axel. Look. Look over there. I can see a living creature like ourselves, a man!'

At first I did not believe him, but when I looked I could see he was right. There, less than a quarter of a mile away, leaning against a tree, was a human being, a man, watching the mastodons.

The Tunnel

But this was not a man like the skeletons we had found back on the sea shore. This was a giant, over twelve feet tall, with a head as big as a cow's, and hair on it like that of a lion.

We had not moved since we saw him, but he might see us. We must run.

'Come on, come on!' I urged my uncle. For the first time in his life, he listened to persuasion.

A quarter of an hour later, we were out of sight of the enemy.

Was it a man we saw? Now, months later, I can't believe that it was. No human being could exist in that underground world. The idea is mad. However, at the time, we ran, silent with amazement, back towards the Lidenbrock Sea.

Luckily we had something else to worry about besides giants. Sometimes, on our way, we saw things that reminded us of Port Grauben, and made us think that we had returned to the north shore. At one point, for instance, I thought I recognized our faithful Hansbach, and the cave in which I had returned to life. Then, a few steps further on, everything seemed completely new.

'Clearly,' I said to my uncle, 'the storm has not carried us back to exactly the point from which we set sail. Still, if we follow the coast, we shall probably come to Port Grauben.'

'If that is so,' replied my uncle, 'we might as well return to the raft. But are you sure you're right, Axel?'

'It's hard to be sure, Uncle, because all these rocks look so alike. But I think that may be the harbour where Hans built the raft.'

'No, Axel, if it were, we should at least see some sign of our …'

'But I can!' I shouted, rushing towards something that lay on the sand, and picking it up.

I showed my uncle an old hunting knife which was now red with rust.

'Well, well!' he said. 'So you had this knife when we were here before?'

'No, not I. But you …'

'It's not mine. But Icelanders carry knives of this kind. Hans must have had it and dropped it.'

I shook my head. I had never seen Hans with such a knife.

'Does it belong to that giant, then?' I cried. 'No, it can't. The blade is steel …'

'Calm down, Axel, and try to think more carefully,' interrupted my uncle in his coldest voice. 'Look, it is not a knife, but a dagger. This is a sixteenth century weapon. It belongs neither to you nor to me, nor to Hans, nor to any other human beings who live down here now.'

'You mean …'

'Look at it. We are on the way to a great discovery. That blade has been lying on this sand not for a day, or a year, but for 300 years!'

'But it didn't get here by itself!' I cried. 'Someone has been here before us!'

'Yes, a man.'

'And that man?'

'That man, I believe, has carved his name somewhere, using this dagger. He wanted, once more, to show people the way to the centre of the earth. Let us look around.'

Wildly excited, we searched among the rocks, looking into every crack. Presently we reached a place where the sea came up almost to the bottom of the cliffs. Between two rocks, we saw the entrance to a dark tunnel. And there, carved into the rock, appeared two mysterious letters, the first letters of the bold traveller's name.

'A.S.,' my uncle cried out. 'Arne Saknussemm! Arne Saknussemm again!'

Forward!

At the sight of those two letters, carved 300 years before, I was struck dumb. Yes, after all that had happened to us, I could still be amazed. Not only was I looking at the marks Saknussemm had cut into the rock, but I was also holding the dagger he had used to carve them. Now I had to believe in the man and his journey.

Professor Lidenbrock was busy praising Saknussemm's name.

'Oh, brilliant man!' he cried. 'You have done everything in your power to open, to other men, the road through the earth's crust. Even now, after three centuries, they can follow your footsteps. You have made it possible for other eyes to see these wonders. Your name, carved here and there, shows other bold travellers the way, and at the centre of the earth it will be found again. Well, I too shall sign my name on that last page of granite. As for these cliffs beside this sea which was first discovered by you, let them be known as Cape Saknussemm!'

When I heard my uncle speaking like this, my own interest came flooding back. I forgot the dangers of the journey so far, and those dangers still to come. What another man had done, I would do too.

'Forward! Forward!' I cried.

I was already rushing towards the tunnel when, surprisingly, the Professor stopped me.

'Let us go back to Hans first,' he said, 'and bring the raft here.'

I had to agree, and we started back along the shore.

'Uncle,' I said as we walked, 'we have really been very lucky so far.'

'You think so, Axel?'

'Yes, I do. Even that storm was lucky for us. Fine weather was taking us to the southern shore of the

Lidenbrock Sea, where we should have been lost. The storm brought us back here, where we found the name of Saknussemm.'

'Yes, Axel, I must say it does seem fortunate, but I can't find any way to explain it.'

'What does that matter? Our business is not to explain facts but to take advantage of them. And now we are going north again, under the northern countries of Europe, instead of crawling under the deserts of Africa or something. That's all I need to know.'

'Yes, Axel, you are right. Everything seems to be working out well. We are leaving this horizontal sea that could lead us nowhere and now we shall go down, down, down. Do you realize we're now less than 4,000 miles from the centre?'

'Is that all?' I cried. 'Why, that's nothing. Let's go!'

We were still having this crazy conversation when we got back to Hans. Everything was ready, and we sailed straight for Cape Saknussemm.

At about six in the evening, after three hours' slow sailing, we arrived. I jumped out onto the sand, followed by the others. I was still just as eager. I even suggested burning the raft to make going back impossible. But my uncle refused. I thought him very unadventurous.

'At least,' I said, 'let's start without delay.'

'Yes, my boy. But let us look into the tunnel first, to see if we shall need our rope ladders.'

The Professor took his lamp, and I led the way to the opening, twenty yards away. It was about five feet across and level with the ground, so we were able to enter without difficulty. After about six steps, however, the way was blocked by a huge rock.

'Oh, no!' I shouted angrily.

We looked to right and left, and up and down, for a way through. There was no gap.

Disappointed, I sat down on the ground. My uncle marched backwards and forwards.

'But what about Saknussemm?' I cried.

'Yes,' said my uncle, 'was he stopped by this rock?'

'No, no!' I exclaimed. 'It must have fallen after his return to the surface. Perhaps it was loosened during a storm like the one we met. Anyhow, if we don't move it, we are not fit to reach the centre of the earth.'

That was how I spoke! The Professor's feelings had passed straight on to me. I forgot the past, and had no interest in the future. Nothing existed on the surface for me any longer, neither Hamburg, nor King's Street, nor even my poor little Grauben.

'Well,' said my uncle, 'let us break it with our axes.'

'It's too hard for axes,' I replied.

'Then what?'

'Gunpowder, of course. We'll blow it up!'

'Hans! To work!' cried my uncle.

The Icelander returned to the raft to fetch an axe and the gunpowder.

'We shall get through!' I said in high excitement.

'We shall get through,' repeated my uncle.

By midnight, our preparations were finished. Hans had made a hole in the rock to hold the gunpowder. All that was needed was one tiny flame and …

'Tomorrow,' said the Professor. I had to wait another six long hours.

The explosion

The next day, Thursday 27th August, was a turning-point in our journey. Even now, I remember it with terror.

At six o'clock we woke up. It was time to blow up the granite.

I made a fuse from a length of string, into which I rubbed a small amount of gunpowder. Then I laid it along the floor of the tunnel, from the granite rock to the entrance. I estimated that it would burn for ten minutes before reaching the rock. There would be plenty of time to light it and run back to safety.

We had a quick breakfast first, and then my uncle and Hans went on board the raft, while I stayed on the shore with a lantern.

'Off you go, my boy,' said the Professor, 'and come straight back here after you have lit the fuse.'

'Don't worry,' I replied, 'I won't stop to play!'

I went to the tunnel entrance, opened the lantern and picked up the end of the fuse. The Professor was holding his chronometer.

'Ready?' he called out.

'Yes, I'm ready.'

'Then fire, my boy!'

I held the end of the fuse in the flame, saw it light up, and ran back to the edge of the water.

'On board,' said my uncle, 'and let's go!'

Hans pushed the loaded raft about sixty feet out to sea.

It was an exciting moment. The Professor was watching his chronometer.

'Another five minutes,' he said. 'Another four ... three ... two ... one ... Now, you granite mountain, down you go!'

What happened then? I don't think I heard the noise of the explosion. But the rocks opened like a curtain before my eyes. An enormous hole opened up in the shore itself. The sea seemed to turn into one huge wave, on top of which stood our raft. Down into the hole went the wave, taking our raft with it.

All three of us were thrown flat on our faces. There was complete darkness. There seemed to be nothing underneath the raft at all. The roar of the water was too loud for us to speak, but I realized what had happened. Behind the rock we had just blown up, there was an abyss. And the sea was now pouring into it, carrying us too.

I gave up all hope.

We seemed to be going down almost vertically and very, very fast.

Our second battery lamp had been broken in the explosion but suddenly Hans managed to light the lantern. The flame was unsteady but it helped a little in the frightening darkness.

The tunnel had indeed opened out. In the dim lantern light, we could not see both sides at once. I estimated that we were travelling down between them at something like eighty miles an hour.

My uncle and I looked around in despair, hanging on to what remained of the mast and turning our backs to the rush of air. The hours went by. I discovered that of our instruments, only the compass and chronometer remained. Of our equipment, there was only one piece of rope tied around the broken mast. Worst of all, the only food left was a piece of salt meat and a few biscuits.

Bravely, I did not tell my uncle this latest horror. I wanted him to stay cool and in control.

And at that moment, the lantern went out. Hans was not able to light it again as the air was rushing past us too violently. Like a child, I closed my eyes to avoid looking into all that darkness.

Down and down we fell, the water from the Lidenbrock sea dropping with us as we went. My uncle and Hans held me firmly by the arms while our little raft carried all three of us towards the centre of the earth.

Eruption

The compass goes mad

I suppose it was about ten o'clock that night, when I noticed it was quiet. The roar of the water had suddenly stopped.

'We are going up!' my uncle shouted. 'We are, we are going up!'

I stretched out my arm and touched the wall, hurting my hand. We were rising extremely fast.

'The lamp! The lamp!' cried the Professor.

With some difficulty, Hans lit it.

'I thought so,' said my uncle. 'We are in a passage about twenty feet across. The water has reached the bottom of the abyss and has pushed us into a side passage. It is now levelling out, rising and taking us with it.'

'Taking us where?'

'I don't know but we must be ready for anything. We are rising at about twelve feet a second, or about eight miles an hour. At this rate, we shall go a long way.'

'Yes,' I said, 'so long as this passage has an opening. If not, we shall be crushed when we reach the end of it.'

'Axel,' said the Professor very calmly, 'we may die at any moment but, equally, we may be saved at any moment. Let us be ready to seize any chance.'

'But what shall we do now?'

'Eat to make ourselves strong.'

'Eat?' I repeated. Now he had to be told.

'What?' cried my uncle. 'All our food gone?'

'Yes, except one piece of meat. Do you still think we can be saved?' He did not reply.

An hour passed. We all began to feel hungry, but none of us dared to touch that last bit of food.

Meanwhile, we were still rising very fast. And the temperature was rising, too. At that point, it must have been 40°C. In spite of Humphry Davy, Otto Lidenbrock and all that had happened to us so far, I still believed in the theory of central heat. Were we finally coming to a place where the heat reduced rock to liquid?

'If we are neither drowned nor crushed, and if we don't die of hunger,' I said to the Professor, 'we may still be burnt alive.'

Again, he did not reply. Another hour passed, during which the temperature rose slightly. At last my uncle spoke, 'If we suddenly get a chance to save ourselves, how shall we be able to take it, if we are weak from hunger?'

'Then you haven't given up hope?' I cried.

'Certainly not,' the Professor replied in a firm voice. 'No creature with will-power should ever despair.'

What splendid words! The man was extraordinary.

'Then what do you suggest we do?'

'Eat all the food that is left. This may be our last meal but at least we shall have the strength to live through the next few hours.'

'Very well. Let us eat,' I agreed.

My uncle divided the meat and biscuits equally into three, and gave each of us our share. The Professor ate his with a sort of greedy excitement. I ate without pleasure in spite of my hunger. Hans ate quietly and slowly, calmly enjoying each mouthful. He had found half a bottle of gin, which he offered around.

'Very good,' said Hans, drinking.

'Excellent' said my uncle.

A little hope had returned to me. But our last meal was soon over. It was five in the morning, and we were silent again.

I wondered what Hans was thinking. For my part, I thought of the house on King's Street which I should never have left, of poor Grauben and dear old Martha.

Now the temperature was rising fast. We had to take off our jackets.

'Are we going up into a furnace?' I cried.

'Impossible, impossible!' replied my uncle.

'All the same,' I said, feeling the side, 'this wall is burning hot.'

My hand touched the water too and I quickly removed it.

'The water is boiling!' I cried.

The Professor shook his head at me angrily.

Then terror seized me. An idea formed in my mind which I did not dare put into words. Everything I saw made me more and more certain that I was right. By the light of the lamp, I saw that the granite wall of the passage was slowly beginning to move. Add to that the heat, the boiling water ... I decided to look at the compass. It had gone mad!

Yes, the compass had gone mad. The needle was swinging around to every point in turn.

And that wasn't all. There were loud explosions, more and more of them, until the noise was like continuous thunder.

I was right. The whole mineral crust was going to burst apart and crush us.

'Uncle, Uncle,' I cried. 'This is the end!'

'What's the matter now?' he replied calmly.

'What's the matter? Look at these shaking walls, this heat, this boiling water, this crazy needle — all the signs of an earthquake!'

My uncle shook his head gently.

'An earthquake?' he asked.

'Yes!'

'My boy, I don't think you're right.'

'What! Don't you recognize the signs?'

'Of an earthquake? No. I am expecting something better than that.'

'What do you mean?'

'It's an eruption, Axel.'

'An eruption? You mean you think we are inside a volcano?'

'I do,' said the Professor with a smile, 'and I'm delighted.'

Delighted? Had my uncle gone crazy, too?

'What!' I exclaimed. 'We are caught in the middle of an eruption. We are in the path of burning lava and boiling water. We are going to be thrown out into the air among rocks and flames. And you say you are delighted!'

'Yes,' replied the Professor, looking at me over the top of his glasses. 'Because it's our only chance of returning to the surface.'

He was right, of course, absolutely right. And never had he seemed bolder than at that moment, when he was calmly weighing the possibility of being caught in an eruption.

We continued to rise. Night came, and we were still going up, with the noise around us getting louder all the time.

We were in the chimney of a volcano, that was certain. But this time, instead of being extinct like Sneffels, it was active. Under the raft was boiling water and under that, a whole lot of lava and rocks, which would be thrown in all directions when they were shot out of the crater. We were about to die — yet I started wondering in what part of the world we would reach the surface. I was sure it would be somewhere in the north. Before the compass had gone mad, it had shown we were going north. From Cape Saknussemm we had been carried north for hundreds of miles. Were we now under Iceland again? Would we be shot out of one of its eight volcanoes?

Towards morning, we began to move faster. Now I noticed deep tunnels on both sides of us, pouring out steam and flame.

'Look, Uncle, look!' I cried, pointing at them. 'What if we choke?'

'We won't. The chimney is getting wider.'

'And what about the rising water?'

'There's no water now, Axel. It's a sort of lava paste that is carrying us up.'

The liquid column had indeed changed into a sort of boiling paste that was carrying us to the mouth of the crater. By now, the temperature must have been over 70°C.

Back to the surface

At about eight in the morning, something new happened. We suddenly stopped rising and the raft lay quite still. Was it caught on something? No, the paste column itself had stopped moving.

'Has the eruption finished?' I cried.

'Ah, my boy,' said my uncle, 'you are afraid that it has, aren't you? But don't worry. Before long, we shall start moving again.'

The Professor watched his chronometer as he spoke. Once again he was proved right. Soon the raft started moving and rose fast for about two minutes. Then it stopped again.

'Good,' said my uncle. 'Ten minutes from now it will start again. This is a volcano which has regular small eruptions with short pauses between them — allowing us to recover our breath!'

How many times it happened, I cannot say. For a few minutes the raft would shoot upwards, with such force that the burning air took my breath away. Then, for ten minutes it would stop, while we nearly choked with the heat.

I thought how wonderful it would be suddenly to find myself in the snow. I imagined myself rolling in the cold white snow of the North Pole. More than once, as my brain weakened, Hans's arms saved me from being crushed against the side of the tunnel.

During the hours that followed, I remember only continuous explosions, moving rocks, and the raft turning round and round. It rocked on waves of lava, it was surrounded by roaring flames. A hurricane seemed to be blowing across the underground fires.

For the last time, I saw Hans's face in the flames. Then came all the terror of the final explosion. I felt like a man tied to the mouth of a big gun just as the shot is fired.

When I opened my eyes again, I was lying on a mountain slope. Hans's strong hand held my belt. With his other hand, he was supporting my uncle. I was not seriously hurt, though I was scratched all over.

'Where are we?' asked my uncle, who seemed extremely annoyed at being back on the surface of the earth.

'In Iceland,' I said.

'No,' said Hans.

'What, not in Iceland?' cried the Professor.

I sat up. After all the surprises of our journey, here was one more. I expected to see a peak covered with snow but my uncle, the Icelander and I were lying half-way down a mountain baked by the rays of a very hot sun.

I could not believe my eyes. I wanted to be in Iceland at least, and I would accept nothing else. The Professor was the first to speak.

'It certainly doesn't look like Iceland,' he said. 'This is no northern volcano with a snow-covered top.'

'All the same ... '

'Look, Axel, look!'

Above our heads, 500 feet up, there was a volcano erupting every quarter of an hour. Below us, streams of lava stretched for about 800 feet. At the base of the mountain grew olive trees, and plants heavy with purple fruit.

I had to admit that this was no land of snow. I looked further and saw that we were on a magic island, set in a lovely sea. To our east was a little harbour with a few houses, and fishing boats rocking on its blue waves. In the distance were more small islands, more mountains. To the north, a great sheet of water glittered in the sun.

It was beautiful, and even more beautiful because it was so unexpected.

'Where are we? Where are we?' I kept asking.

Hans closed his eyes, not caring.

'Wherever we are,' said my uncle, 'it's rather hot, and the eruption is still going on. It would be a pity to come safely out of a volcano and then be hit on the head by a piece of rock. Let's go down out of the way. Anyhow, I'm dying of hunger and thirst.'

I could have stayed there for hours, but I had to follow my companions. The sides of the volcano were steep, but I talked away in my excitement, 'We are in Asia!' I cried. 'We must be on the coast of India or Malaya ... '

'But what about the compass?' said my uncle.

'Yes, of course, the compass,' I said, puzzled. 'According to the compass, we were travelling north all the time.'

'Then was it lying?'

'Lying? No, how could it?'

'Then this is the North Pole?'

'The Pole? No, but ... '

There was a mystery here and I did not know what to think — except that I was feeling hungry, too.

The blue skies of Sicily

Fortunately, after walking for two hours, we reached a lovely place, full of fruit trees. What a delight it was to bite off whole bunches of fruit, and to drink from a spring of fresh water!

While we were thus enjoying ourselves, a small boy appeared between the trees. The sight of three strangers with long, untidy beards, and with their clothes all torn and dirty, frightened him and he tried to run away. Hans caught him and brought him back to us, kicking and screaming.

'What is the name of this mountain?' my uncle asked him kindly in German.

The child did not answer.

'Good,' said my uncle, 'we are not in Germany.'

He then asked the same question in English.

Still the child did not answer.

'Is the boy dumb?' cried the Professor. Proud of his knowledge of languages, he repeated the question in French.

The same silence.

'Then let's try Italian,' said my uncle, and asked his question again.

'Stromboli,' said the boy and ran off through the trees.

Stromboli! We were in the middle of the Mediterranean!

'Stromboli! Stromboli!' I repeated.

'Stromboli!' cried my uncle.

Oh, what a journey! What a wonderful journey! We had gone in by one volcano and come out by another, more than 3,000 miles away. We had exchanged Sneffels for Stromboli, the grey fog of Iceland for the blue skies of the island of Sicily, in the centre of the Mediterranean Sea!

We set off for the port, and on the way I heard my uncle muttering, 'But the compass! The compass! It said north! How can we explain that?'

'Why bother to explain it?' I said.

'What! A Professor at the Johannaeum unable to explain something! What a terrible idea!'

As he spoke, dressed in rags, but putting his glasses firmly on his nose, my uncle became once more the well-known Professor of Mineralogy.

An hour later, we reached the port of San Vicenzo, where Hans received his thirteenth week's wages. My uncle gave them to him and we both shook his hand.

At that moment, something extraordinary happened. The Icelander smiled.

Home again

We told the Stromboli fishermen that we had been shipwrecked. We thought the truth would have frightened them.

They were very kind to us. They gave us food and clothing and, on 31st August, a small boat took us to Messina.

Here we rested until Friday 4th September, when we sailed on a French boat to Marseilles. Our only worry by this time was the compass. Its strange behaviour bothered me all the way to Hamburg, where we arrived on the evening of 9th September.

I won't try to describe Martha's amazement and Grauben's joy at our return.

'Now that you are a hero,' said my little Grauben, 'you will never need to leave me again.' She smiled at me through her tears.

In Hamburg, Professor Lidenbrock's return caused great excitement. Thanks to Martha, the whole world knew that he had set off for the centre of the earth. People had refused to believe it, and when they saw him again, they still refused to believe it. Gradually, however, when they saw Hans, and heard from Iceland about our visit there, they changed their minds.

My uncle then became a great man, and I became the nephew of a great man.

Hamburg gave a dinner in his honour. A public meeting was held at the Johannaeum, at which the Professor told the story of his expedition (leaving out only the mystery of the compass). He gave Saknussemm's parchment to the city, and said he was sorry that he had not been able to follow him right to the centre of the earth.

He defended his theory that the central parts of the earth were cool, before scientists from all over the world. For my part, I could not agree with him here. In spite of what we saw, I believed, and still do believe, in the idea of a hot centre.

At this point, something very sad happened to both of us. Hans left Hamburg. The man to whom we owed our lives would not stay any longer as our guest. He wanted to be back in Iceland.

'Goodbye,' he said one day, and returned to Reykjavik. We shall never forget our bird-hunter.

I should add that this *Journey to the Centre of the Earth* became world-famous. It appeared in all languages and was eagerly discussed, attacked and defended, through the newspapers in many different countries. My uncle enjoyed great fame for the rest of his life.

But for a while, one thing spoilt his happiness. He didn't understand the behaviour of the compass and, to a scientist, something unexplained is a constant annoyance.

One day, about six months after our return, while I was arranging a collection of minerals in the Professor's study, I noticed the famous compass lying in a corner. I cried out in surprise. Professor Lidenbrock came running in.

'What's the matter?' he asked.

'The compass!'

'Well?'

'Look! The needle points south instead of north!'

My uncle looked, compared the compass with another and then gave a leap of joy which shook the house. The mystery was solved.

'So,' he exclaimed as soon as he could speak again, 'after our arrival at Cape Saknussemm, the needle of this compass pointed south instead of north?'

'Clearly.'

'Then that explains our mistake. By following the compass we thought we had been going north, but we were really heading south. But why did it do it?'

'It's all very simple.'

'Explain yourself, my boy.'

'During the storm on the Lidenbrock Sea,' I said, 'that fire-ball which magnetized all the iron on the raft also changed the poles of our compass.'

'Ah-ha!!' cried the Professor, bursting into laughter. 'So it was a trick that the electricity played on us!'

From that day, my uncle was the happiest of scientists. And I was the happiest of men, for my pretty Grauben took her place in the King's Street house as both wife and god-daughter. Her godfather, of course, was the famous Professor Otto Lidenbrock.

QUESTIONS AND ACTIVITIES

CHAPTER 1

Put these words in the right gaps: ***fanning, sense, key, letters, grouping, code, backwards, rushed, impossible, towards, picked, read, back.***

Professor Lidenbrock tried to find the key to the (1) _____ for the words on the parchment. He read out the (2) _____ of the words going down the page. But that made no (3) _____. He struck the table and (4) _____ out. I (5) _____ up the paper on which I had written the letters. I tried (6) _____ them to form words. It was (7) _____. I started (8) _____ myself with the paper. As the (9) _____ of the paper was turned (10) _____ me, I thought I could (11) _____ more Latin words. I had found the (12) _____! The paper could be read just as it was — but (13) _____.

CHAPTER 2

Who said these words? Choose from: ***Martha, Mr Fridriksson, Axel, Grauben, Professor Lidenbrock.***

1 'It will be a wonderful journey. I would gladly come with you if I could.'
2 'Of course we must go now! Do you think it's so easy to get to Iceland?'
3 'Is the master mad? And he's taking you with him?'
4 'But when we have gone down, we still have to come up again.'
5 'I want to find the works of Arne Saknussemm.'
6 'Now I see why Saknussemm had to hide his secret.'
7 'There are so many mountains, glaciers and volcanoes still to be studied.'

...e words in the right order.

... to Sneffels now. We stopped for the night in ... Stapi, and the (2) **wonflilog** day we did not ... (3) **treeghyniv** ready for our long (4) **yorjune** ...rth. I had almost forgotten my fear during the (5) ...**intex** of travelling, but now it (6) **deisez** me again. I worn... that Sneffels might not really be (7) **tentcix**, and that a new (8) **poturien** might happen at any (9) **nemmot**. My uncle would not (10) **slenit** to me.

CHAPTER 4

Put these sentences in the right order to say what happened in this part of the story. The first one is done for you.

1 My uncle took a rope which was 400 feet long and thick as a thumb.
2 After three hours, I still couldn't see the bottom of the chimney.
3 After ten and a half hours, we reached the bottom, 2,800 feet down.
4 He passed it around a lava block, and threw the ends down the chimney.
5 After half an hour, we reached a large rock fixed to the chimney wall.
6 Hans pulled one end of the rope, and the other came down from the top.
7 Then it was our turn, so we put on our packs and the descent began.
8 Hans tied the clothes and ropes in a bundle and threw them down too.

CHAPTER 5

There are 12 mistakes in this paragraph. Can you find them?

We went down the eastern passage, looking for water. At eight o'clock, there were signs of water. My eyes began to fail. I tried

QUESTIONS AND ACT.

to keep awake, but finally I yawned and sat down. .
expression of happiness was the last thing I saw before I c.
my door. When I opened it again, I saw my three enemies lying
rolled up in their clothes. A few days passed: Then I saw the
Frenchman going into a nearby tunnel.

CHAPTER 6

Which of these sentences are true? What is wrong with the false ones?

1 On Sunday 19th July, my uncle decided to put his daily notes in order.
2 We worked out our exact position to be under the Pacific Ocean.
3 The Professor estimated that we were eight miles below the surface.
4 The temperature ought to have been 1,500°C, but it was only 27.6°C.
5 I said that at this rate, it would take us 1,000 days to reach the centre.
6 My uncle said the density would decrease, and we would get lighter.
7 We would have to fill our pockets with stones in order to continue.

CHAPTER 7

Choose the right words to say what this part of the story is about.

Water, the beginning of a (1) **lake/pond** or an ocean, stretched away out of (2) **the cave/sight**. There was a (3) **flat/sloping** beach of fine, (4) **golden/black** sand, covered with (5) **huge/small** shells. Behind it, a line of (6) **cliffs/volcanoes** curved up to great (7) **lengths/heights**. It was empty and (8) **gentle/wild** in appearance. The light was neither warm like the (9) **sun/lamps**, nor cold like that of the (10) **stars/moon**. It was a (11) **weak/strong**, (12) **white/yellow** light, that was clearly (13) **gas/electric**.

Chapter 10

Put these words in the right gaps: **blown, flame, realized, wave, edge, abyss, fuse, curtain, pouring, darkness, tunnel, enormous, nothing.**

It was time to blow up the granite rock. I made a (1) _____ and laid it along the floor of the (2) _____. I held the end of it in the (3) _____, saw it light up, and ran back to the (4) _____ of the water. Then the rocks opened like a (5) _____ before my eyes. An (6) _____ hole opened up in the shore itself. The sea seemed to turn into one huge (7) _____. Down into the hole it went, taking our raft with it. There was complete (8) _____, and there seemed to be (9) _____ under the raft at all. I (10) _____ what had happened. Behind the rock we had just (11) _____ up was an (12) _____. And the sea was now (13) _____ into it, carrying us too.

Chapter 11

Put the right beginnings with the right endings.

1 The temperature was 40°C and
2 Soon the wall was burning hot and
3 I saw that the wall was moving and
4 I thought it was an earthquake, but
5 He said it was something earthquake, but
6 He said he was delighted and
7 Then he said it was our only chance

(a) an eruption inside a volcano.
(b) of returning to the surface.
(c) I thought he had gone crazy.
(d) the water was boiling.
(e) the compass had gone mad.
(f) we were still rising very fast.
(g) my uncle didn't think so.

Grade 1

Alice's Adventures in Wonderland
Lewis Carroll

The Call of the Wild and Other Stories
Jack London

Emma
Jane Austen

The Golden Goose and Other Stories
Retold by David Foulds

Jane Eyre
Charlotte Brontë

Just So Stories
Rudyard Kipling

Little Women
Louisa M. Alcott

The Lost Umbrella of Kim Chu
Eleanor Estes

The Secret Garden
Frances Hodgson Burnett

Tales From the Arabian Nights
Edited by David Foulds

Treasure Island
Robert Louis Stevenson

The Wizard of Oz
L. Frank Baum

Grade 2

The Adventures of Sherlock Holmes
Sir Arthur Conan Doyle

A Christmas Carol
Charles Dickens

The Dagger and Wings and Other Father Brown Stories
G.K. Chesterton

The Flying Heads and Other Strange Stories
Edited by David Foulds

The Golden Touch and Other Stories
Edited by David Foulds

Gulliver's Travels — A Voyage to Lilliput
Jonathan Swift

The Jungle Book
Rudyard Kipling

Life Without Katy and Other Stories
O. Henry

Lord Jim
Joseph Conrad

A Midsummer Night's Dream and Other Stories from Shakespeare's Plays
Edited by David Foulds

Oliver Twist
Charles Dickens

The Mill on the Floss
George Eliot

Nicholas Nickleby
Charles Dickens

The Prince and the Pauper
Mark Twain

The Stone Junk and Other Stories
D.H. Howe

Stories from Greek Tragedies
Retold by Kieran McGovern

Stories from Shakespeare's Comedies
Retold by Katherine Mattock

Tales of King Arthur
Retold by David Foulds

The Talking Tree and Other Stories
David McRobbie

Through the Looking Glass
Lewis Carroll

Grade 3

The Adventures of Huckleberry Finn
Mark Twain

The Adventures of Tom Sawyer
Mark Twain

Around the World in Eighty Days
Jules Verne

The Canterville Ghost and Other Stories
Oscar Wilde

David Copperfield
Charles Dickens

Fog and Other Stories
Bill Lowe

Further Adventures of Sherlock Holmes
Sir Arthur Conan Doyle

Great Expectations
Charles Dickens

Gulliver's Travels — Further Voyages
Jonathan Swift